THE CLASSROOM OBSERVER

Developing Observation Skills
in Early Childhood Settings

SECOND EDITION

THE CLASSROOM OBSERVER

Developing Observation Skills
in Early Childhood Settings

SECOND EDITION

ANN E. BOEHM
RICHARD A. WEINBERG

TEACHERS
COLLEGE
PRESS

Teachers College, Columbia University
New York and London

The first edition of this book appeared in 1977 under the title, *The Classroom Observer: A Guide for Developing Observation Skills.*

Text photographs by Myron Papiz.

Published by Teachers College Press, 1234 Amsterdam Avenue,
New York, NY 10027

Library of Congress Cataloging-in-Publication Data

Boehm, Ann E., 1938–
   The classroom observer.

   Bibliography: p. 141
   Includes index.
   1. Observation (Educational method)   2. Child
development.   3. Education, Primary.   I. Weinberg,
Richard A.   II. Title.
LB1027.28.B64   1987   371.11'46   87-18036
ISBN 0-8077-2874-8 (pbk.)

Manufactured in the United States of America

92 91 90 89   2 3 4 5 6

*To
Gail and Neville,
again*

Contents

LIST OF TASKS   xi

PREFACE   xiii

UNIT I   **AN INTRODUCTION TO THE SKILLS
           OF OBSERVATION**   1

           Observing in the Early Childhood Arena   2
           Observing Systematically   4

UNIT II   **APPLYING OBSERVATION SKILLS
           TO LEARNING SETTINGS**   6

           Observation as a Method of Inquiry   6
           Observation Techniques in Studying Child
                 Development   8
           Observing Within the Educational Environment   10

UNIT III   **THE FORMS OF OBSERVATION**   16

           Diary Descriptions   16
           Anecdotal Records   16
           Specimen Records   17
           Checklists   20
           Rating Scales   20
           Formal Observation Schedules   23

UNIT IV   **THE SELECTIVE NATURE OF OUR OBSERVATIONS**   25

           Subjectivity in Observation   27
           Aiming for Objectivity in Our Observations   28
           The Effect of the Observer's Presence   31
           Drawing Inferences   32

**UNIT V   DEFINING THE PROBLEM AND DESCRIBING
              THE SETTING**   **37**

              Defining the Problem   38
              The Constraints of the Setting   39
              Analyzing the Components of the Setting   42
              The Context of Behavior   46

UNIT VI   LABELING AND CATEGORIZING BEHAVIOR   **51**

              Dimensions for Labeling Behaviors   51
              Mutually Exclusive and Exhaustive Categories   53
              Specifying Categories   56
              Category and Sign Systems   58
              Developing Categories   60

**UNIT VII   MAKING RELIABLE OBSERVATIONS:
              AVOIDING OBSERVATIONAL BIAS**   **62**

              Obtaining Reliable Observations   62
              Challenges to Reliable Observations   67

UNIT VIII SAMPLING AND RECORDING BEHAVIOR   **71**

              What's to Be Observed   71
              Recording Observational Data   79
              Other Recording Formats   83
              Making Valid Observations   86
              Determining the Appropriateness
                of an Observation System   89
              Ethical Issues in Observation   91

UNIT IX   THE TEACHER AS OBSERVER   **93**

              The Teacher or the Outsider as Observer   93
              Solving Classroom Problems through
                Observation Techniques   95
              Studying Developmental Differences in Children   97
              Steps to Making Classroom Observations   100

**UNIT X   THE RELATIONSHIP BETWEEN MEDIA
              AND OBSERVATION**   **107**

              The "Mechanics" of Media and the Observer   107
              Advantages and Disadvantages of the Media
                of Observation   109

UNIT XI   **DEVELOPING OBSERVATION METHODS**
APPROPRIATE TO THE COMPUTER-ASSISTED
LEARNING ENVIRONMENT   **115**

Computer-Assisted Tutoring: Use of
    Computer Software   116
Forms of Observation Useful in the Computer
    Environment   117
Developing an Observational Procedure
    for Computer-Assisted Tutoring   117
Outcomes of Observing Computer-Assisted Tutoring   119

CONCLUSION   121

APPENDIX: SAMPLE RESPONSES TO TASKS   123

REFERENCES   131

BIBLIOGRAPHY   141

INDEX   147

List of Tasks

Task 1   Observations of Your Present Setting   25
Task 2   Observations of a Supermarket Scene   27
Task 3   Distinguishing Objective from Subjective
                or Interpretive Observations   30
Task 4   Observations of a Girl in a Nursery Class   33
Task 5   Differentiating Clearly Stated from Poorly Stated
                Questions   39
Task 6   Constraints Imposed by the Setting   41
Task 7   Visible Characteristics of Individuals   45
Task 8   Key Components of a Setting   46
Task 9   Distinguishing Mutually Exclusive Categories   54
Task 10   Establishing Exhaustive Categories   55
Task 11   Determining Representative Observational Samples   78

Preface

Historically, naturalistic observational techniques have been central to the development of the physical sciences, helping to generate theories and establish knowledge about physical phenomena. Rooted in the rich tradition of the physical sciences, the social sciences have also opened our window of understanding about the social world through the use of systematic observational methods. Skill in observing children has been a cornerstone of the work of "child watchers," those professionals devoted to child study and to understanding why children develop and behave in the ways they do. Appreciating this heritage, we have developed an updated edition of *The Classroom Observer: A Guide for Developing Observation Skills* (first published in 1977), now subtitled, *Developing Observation Skills in Early Childhood Settings*. The program presented in this second edition focuses on those skills needed in order for an early childhood observer to make appropriate, valid inferences and to arrive at decisions based on objective observation data which can be gathered in natural learning habitats and educational settings. This book is based on the premise that observation skills are an indispensable component of an early childhood educator's professional repertoire. Educators are applied empiricists, and are therefore most effective when they have access to sound data to support their planning, interventions, and follow-up efforts.

Although observation is recognized as an important tool for gaining information, drawing conclusions, and generating ideas, limited attention has been devoted to many of the key issues surrounding the effective application of systematic observation in learning environments. The aim of this book is to present critical components that need to be considered in developing systematic observation skills when working in early childhood settings. A major focus is also placed on *self-made* observation strategies rather than on "canned" products. To accomplish these goals, the reader is asked to engage in a series of tasks to develop an understanding of the various principles and procedures introduced. Sample responses are provided for many of these tasks in an appendix, so that the reader can compare his or her answers.

The increasing availability of observation techniques for various professionals involved in the early childhood educational enterprise does not guarantee the development and assimilation of observation skills in training programs for teachers, special educators, health educators, school psychologists, social workers, and other school personnel devoted to the welfare of young children.

Observing children in educational contexts and preparing case studies have been integral components of the training of some individuals engaged in preschool and elementary education (Cohen, Stern, & Balaban, 1983; Good & Brophy, 1984). However, our experience in directing in-service workshops for child care providers, practicing teachers, special educators, and school psychologists has indicated that a step-by-step program for developing objective observation skills is essential if adequate naturalistic observation techniques are to be acquired. Such programs can be incorporated into teacher and other professional training programs as well as in-service and continuing education opportunities. Field experiences and observation practice supplementary to traditional course work and student–teacher experiences can generate interesting seminar discussions about the role of observation in the early childhood education process. The adjunct use of videotaped classroom scenes can provide exercises in studying such concepts as observer reliability, the procedures for generating categories of behavior, and the strategies that children use to solve problems.

Multidisciplinary workshops (including team teachers, student teachers, classroom paraprofessionals, and supportive pupil personnel such as school social workers and psychologists) that explore observational techniques can stress the value of a "team" approach to observing early childhood settings. By sharing their observational data, early childhood personnel can facilitate optimal educational programming. It should become obvious that by extending observational training to educational programs for effective parenting, one can generalize the value of systematic observation skills to the home and family situations. Furthermore, introducing parent observers in the classroom and other early childhood settings might stimulate communication about young children. Older students, too, can be productive observers who might benefit by training in systematic observation.

This second edition is a more expanded volume that maintains its focus on systematic observational skill building in early childhood environments. This edition includes:

1. A new unit on reliability and sources of bias in observation
2. A new unit on observation in media-based learning settings

3. A new unit on the forms of observation
4. A helpful subject/author index
5. Updated references and resources

Although the primary target of our book is the community of professionals who study young children, the audience of educators, researchers, and human service providers who work with older populations should find this quite a useful addition to their resources.

The development of the first and second editions of this volume has been a rewarding experience. We are especially appreciative of Millie Almy who provided us with the initial impetus to write the book. Since the first edition was published, Byron Egeland, Erna Fishhaut, and Shirley Moore of the University of Minnesota and Margaret Jo Shepherd and Leslie R. Williams of Teachers College, Columbia University, have provided us with support and encouragement. John Swayze and Karen Brobst helped in important ways in the development of Units X and XI, respectively. We also appreciate the suggestions and feedback from the students and teachers who employed the first edition in their studies. In addition, we are grateful for the excellent editorial assistance provided by Patrick Lee in the first edition, and by Audrey Kingstrom and Nina George of Teachers College Press in this revision. Finally, we offer thanks to the hundreds of young children in many learning settings whom we have observed and from whom we have learned.

Ann E. Boehm
Richard A. Weinberg

THE CLASSROOM OBSERVER

Developing Observation Skills
in Early Childhood Settings

SECOND EDITION

An Introduction to the Skills of Observation

Today's world demands that each of us make judgments, evaluate situations, and guide our lives on the basis of inferences. Many of these decisions and judgments are based on information that we derive from the environment through observation. We make observations in a variety of settings where we view people behaving in different ways. In our daily observations we take account of the interactions between individuals, the outcomes of interactions, the physical setting in which the exchanges occur, and the nature of the tasks involved. In these various situations the observation process allows us to obtain essential information for drawing inferences and making decisions, unfortunately with varying degrees of validity. We do this in mundane situations, such as inferring that a roast is finished when the meat thermometer registers "rare roast beef" (if we care for rare meat). The observation process also operates in the more consequential areas of our lives:

The coach critically reviews the videotape of the last basketball game and makes a decision as to which team members will start in the next game.

The preschool teacher observes over a two-week period the play patterns of her pupils to evaluate the nature of the interactions among children.

The gymnast watches another competitor compete on the balance beam, observes components of performance not seen by the untrained eye, and makes a list of self-improvement points on which to work during practice.

The radiologist "reads" an X ray for the surgeon, who in turn uses the data as well as the patient's medical history to determine the appropriate surgical technique.

The birdwatcher, the artist, the meteorologist, the farmer, the coin collector, all observe the world through their unique lenses and guide their behavior, decisions, and judgments accordingly.

The level of precision with which one observes events is determined by one's interest, needs, and past experience. Much of what we do or do not see is the result of a casual, nondirected activity. Systematic, scientific observation, however, requires guided observing of consistently observable events.

OBSERVING IN THE EARLY CHILDHOOD ARENA

The early childhood enterprise — educational and child care programs for young children and their families — has long been an arena of debate for parents, educators, behavioral scientists, politicians, and other groups with vested interests in the welfare of young children. Controversy focuses on children's needs, effective strategies for accomplishing educational and developmental goals for individual children, the advantages of varying programs and curricula, and alternative systems for providing services. Furthermore, conflicting political, economic, and social pressures confound the issues. In this climate of unrest and controversy, early childhood professionals, including teachers, administrators, and other specialists, must be all the more deliberate and objective as they go about their business of making inferences, solving daily problems, facilitating the educational process, and generally being accountable for their activities.

New students of observation skills often underestimate the complexities of systematic observation and fail to tap the rich information that is present when viewing a learning situation. For example, an untrained observer entering a kindergarten to observe the "classroom climate" might generate a five-minute "running record" such as:

> Boy crying in block corner.
> Another child angry with his friend who has knocked over his block fort.
> Teacher is ignoring both of these children while a male aide is attempting to intervene in both situations.
> Room seems crowded.
> Art materials are not being used.
> Girls in doll corner are involved in play.

Another observer trained in a systematic approach to making observations would generate a different five-minute "running record" of the same situation: Given the purpose of "observing the classroom climate" the trained observer would develop a simple strategy for observing those components of the setting, child, and teacher behavior that he or she defines ahead of time as components of a "classroom climate." The trained observer systematically takes account of each component by sampling from the situation over the given time period. Such a record might look like this:

Setting and people
There are 15 children present (seven girls, eight boys).
The female teacher is assisted by one male (perhaps a student teacher).
The room is arranged in a variety of activity areas: painting area, doll corner, water table, block area, book area.
Pupil and teacher behavior
The presence of eight semidry paintings hanging on a clothesline suggests that the children were painting earlier.
There are at least two children participating in each of four activity areas (excluding painting).
The teacher is at her desk involved in some "paper activity."
The male (and/or student teacher?) is speaking to the child who is crying in the block area.

Although there is overlap in the "running records" of both the untrained and trained observers, it should be evident that the more systematic approach will permit a stronger basis for arriving at inferences about "the classroom climate" of this particular kindergarten. Specifically, one can note that:

The first running record, by confusing observations with inferences, gives the reader the impression that the overall classroom atmosphere is "unhappy." The second report indicates that the atmosphere is "busy" with an isolated "unhappy" incident.
The second, more systematic report supplies more factual information about the people and the setting.
The first record simply misrepresents the degree of art activity in the room; the second, by taking account of additional information, gives a more valid report.

Thus, although both records provide descriptions of classroom climate, the second, more systematic running record provides us with a more valid representation of the setting.

OBSERVING SYSTEMATICALLY

It is the purpose of this book to provide a systematic approach for observing in learning environments, especially those for young children. The observer, by developing simple observation skills and greater awareness of the valuable tool of observation, can approach the work knowing that decisions and conclusions have been based on a stronger foundation of observation information.

Like the astute political and economic observer, the child observer must be aware of the distorting influences of subjective feelings and intuitive reactions on the observation process. Individuals frequently perceive the same situation differently, their observations reflecting their developmental level, previous experiences, comprehension and understanding of the specific instance, and personal biases. Typical observations tend to reflect individual and egocentric frames of reference, which in turn mirror societal or cultural norms and/or prejudices. A few examples may help to underscore this point:

Individual perceptions
One person reading the *Wall Street Journal* notes, "This paper is dull and uninteresting." However, another person might state, "reading the *Wall Street Journal* provides stimulating information as to the current financial scene."

Cultural norms
A child looks at the floor when he is being taken to task by a teacher. To the child, as a result of his past experiences, this is an indication of deference to and respect for authority. From the standpoint of the teacher, such behavior may be viewed as deviousness, avoidance of confrontation, or admission of guilt.

Developmental influences
The work of Piaget has focused awareness on the fact that, up to about the age of six or seven, children believe all others perceive the world as they do. For example, from her egocentric frame of reference, a child might state that another person, irrespective of his position in the room, sees exactly the same things as she does even if the objects are out of view of the other person.

Approaching a situation, the trained observer uses a systematic strategy for collecting information from the setting. What the observer focuses upon and the pattern of observations that result are not random but are guided by the question posed or the problem needing to be solved. The categories devised for labeling components of the setting, specific people in the observed situation, and behavioral activities that occur are precise and clearly defined.

In collecting and recording observations, the trained observer uses a system that allows a sampling of the situation, taking into account sources of bias. Through a sufficient number of objective observations, he or she is prepared to build valid inferences from a reliable, rich data base of direct observations in natural settings.

Our description of the trained early childhood observer summarizes the various observation skills that this book attempts to foster. The adage "seeing is believing" reflects the powerful role that observation plays in our lives; but it underestimates the advantage that the trained observer has over the naive observer.

Applying Observation Skills to Learning Settings

The program presented in this book is an attempt to demonstrate the role that systematic observation skills can play in one's daily decision-making activities. We have tended to focus on early childhood settings and the observation of young children. However, observation procedures can be used to collect information throughout the educational spectrum, and we have drawn on examples from other educational settings and contexts. This unit provides a brief overview of the role observation methods have played in the study of children's behavior, the educational process, and classroom teaching techniques. It also provides a perspective on how observation techniques can contribute to the efficiency of the teacher, psychologist, special educator, and other personnel involved in education.

OBSERVATION AS A METHOD OF INQUIRY

Historically, objective observation techniques have been central to the scientist's methods of inquiry for generating hypotheses, for building laws of science, and for confirming theories. However, such techniques were not always without difficulty. In fact, Galileo Galilei (1564–1642), the founder of modern astronomy, was condemned by the Church for his use of scientific observation. Having built an astronomical telescope and studied moving bodies in space, he noted that the earth orbited the sun, contrary to the accepted position that the earth was the center of the universe. In this instance, objective data came into direct conflict with a traditional belief that was difficult to refute.

The social sciences, rooted in the tradition of the physical and biological sciences, have also enlarged the scope of human knowledge by deriving conclusions based on objective, observable data. Often, this concern has been limited to the controlled situation of the experimenter's laboratory or the contrived situation of the researcher using questionnaires, rating scales, and clinical testing techniques where observations are made of the effects of an experimenter's manipulations.

The traditional experimental approach emphasizes an artificially controlled manipulation of the environment in order to gain knowledge of various phenomena (e.g., laboratory research in cancer treatment, the study of paired-associate learning behavior of children, the influences of a new curriculum on a child's mastery of a particular subject). The questions raised by the experimenters are these: If we alter the experimental situation in a particular way, what behaviors will result? How will these behaviors compare to those that occur when a different set of environmental conditions is presented? We often forget that observations of our natural "unaltered" environments provide the impetus for laboratory research and stimulate the development of hypotheses, speculations, and researchable ideas. On the other hand, empirical findings in the laboratory often must be verified in naturalistic settings before these results can be accepted.

In contrast, the ecological approach to studying phenomena emphasizes the investigation of observable phenomena as they occur naturally in the environment, uncontrolled by the observer. In reflecting on the ways descriptions of naturally occurring phenomena have contributed to our body of scientific knowledge, Wright (1967) noted:

> Natural history studies have long supplied basic data for the theories and applications of biology. Astronomy and the earth sciences are monuments to investigation that examines at first hand what it finds in nature. All of the social sciences but psychology owe most of their empirical accomplishments to direct recordings of conditions and events in society. Even the predominantly experimental sciences of physics and chemistry have amassed and regularly call upon stores of information about the incidence in nature of their materials and subject processes. Psychology appears to stand alone as a science without a substantial descriptive, naturalistic, ecological side (p. 3).

Sociologists and anthropologists (e.g., Mead, 1932; Parsons & Bales, 1955) have collected field data and used their observational findings in developing much of our understanding about social organizations, the influences of cultural factors on behavior, and the nature of daily living patterns in various groups. Perhaps in response to Wright's critique, psychologists have focused on the ecology of the organism and its environment by exploring behavior in the natural settings of the home, community, or classroom (e.g., Barker, 1968; Barker & Schoggen, 1973; Bronfenbrenner, 1976, 1977).

The valuable work of Barker and Wright at the Kansas Midwest Station has provided a wealth of information, unveiling the natural habitats and behaviors of individuals. *One Boy's Day* (1951) and *Midwest and Its Children: The Psychological Ecology of an American Town*

(1955) illustrate how a descriptive, naturalistic, ecological approach can contribute to our understanding of complex, ongoing human behavior in real life situations, not laboratories. These works have also shown how an observer can accurately record a broad range of natural behavior through the use of specimen records. These in turn generate dimensions of behavior that can be further investigated through the use of other research techniques. Barker and Schoggen (1973) further resolved some conceptual and measurement problems central to studying environments and understanding the links between habitat and behavior. Such understanding enhances our ability to control or predict behavior and to improve the nature and quality of life.

OBSERVATION TECHNIQUES
IN STUDYING CHILD DEVELOPMENT

The earliest systematic observations of children's behavior in natural settings were biographies, diaries, and detailed recordings of children's behavior. One can trace the practice of making diary descriptions or sequential accounts of ongoing activity to the late eighteenth century when many observers kept diaries tracing their children's development. For example, the Swiss educator Johann Pestalozzi (1746–1827) made extensive observations and kept records of the development of his three-and-a-half-year-old son. Other "baby biographies" appeared in the early 1900s, each providing an account of the observed development of a child who was a relative of the biographer. Although these biographies were of value in raising hypotheses about the nature of child development, their generalizability was limited. In addition, the observations were often unsystematic, biased, and selective (Scarr, Weinberg, & Levine, 1986). However, the detailed recordings of observations of children by Jean Piaget (1960), who charted our understanding of the cognitive development of children, and by Roger Brown (1973), who explored the acquisition of language — to cite two well-known examples — were critical underpinnings of the contemporary study of human development. The burgeoning study of human development across the life span from infancy through adulthood in the cognitive, perceptual-motor, social, and emotional domains is built upon the work of these pioneer "child watchers."

Since the early 1970s, there has been an upsurge of interest among developmentalists in extending the ethological approach of studying animal behavior in the natural habitat to investigating children in their natural habitat, such as the home, school, playground, and so on

(Charlesworth, 1978). Ethological research in the biological sciences emphasizes the natural environments of plants and animals as well as the related structure and evolving functions of the living organism. Moving from the domain of the fish pond to the nursery school environment, McGrew (1972) attempted to define "an ethogram for the young *Homo Sapiens*" by observing behavior patterns exhibited by three- and four-year-old children in social situations during nursery-school free play. Focusing on observed children's behavior patterns, such as facial expressions, gestures, postures, and locomotion, McGrew attempted to relate these observations to previous research on human and nonhuman primate behavior.

Observation of parent–child interactions including the development of attachment patterns in infancy, such as the work of Mary Ainsworth (see Ainsworth et al., 1978), has provided another focus for child development researchers. To help clarify the range of observational methods available for studying these interpersonal relationships, Lytton (1971) proposed a hierarchy consisting of observation of structured interaction in the laboratory, observation of unstructured interaction in the laboratory (free play), and naturalistic observation in the home. Components of this hierarchy reflect varying degrees of control over the situation in which observations are collected. Baumrind (1968) has stressed that one must doubt the generalizability of observational data gathered from a rigorously controlled experimental situation to the natural family situation in which the child grows up and is socialized.

In the tradition of ecological investigations of human behavior, Caldwell (1969) proposed an impressive method for translating observational data into a numerical code suitable for computer analysis called the HOME (Home Observation for Measurement of the Environment) Inventory (see Bradley, 1982; Caldwell & Bradley, 1979). Caldwell warned that the formulation of comprehensive theories of early childhood learning and the understanding of patterns of environmental care will require naturalistic studies and descriptions of children functioning in different "freely constituted" environmental settings. A number of other developmental and early childhood researchers have also recognized the problems associated with premature leaps into the laboratory, and have begun to conduct observational studies of naturally occurring behavior events (e.g., Charlesworth, 1978; Landesman-Dwyer, Stein, & Sackett, 1978; White et al., 1973b).

In summary, then, many child development specialists have come to recognize that the naturalistic approach to studying human development contributes a richness, validity, and vitality not usually found in laboratory-based research. If well-planned and carefully controlled, such observations can yield data that are perfectly respectable from a scientific point of view. Moreover, they often suggest hypotheses that can then undergo more intensive examination in laboratory settings. Thus, the full spectrum of observational approaches, ranging from naturalistic observation to laboratory-based observation, should be viewed as complementary rather than as competitive routes to scientifically valid knowledge.

OBSERVING WITHIN THE EDUCATIONAL ENVIRONMENT

The educational environment — its settings, curriculum, and methods — has been the focus of many observation studies. Of particular interest is the role that naturalistic observation has played in the behavior management movement, psychoeducational assessment, the development of criterion-referenced assessment techniques, and the evaluation of curricular programs and teaching effectiveness.

Observation in the Management of Behavior

Influenced by the Skinnerian tradition of behaviorism and learning theory, the findings of social learning research (Baldwin, 1968; Bandura & Walters, 1963), and the pressing need for alternative ways to deal with school behavior and learning problems, educational psychologists and other professionals in education have developed operant conditioning and behavioral management techniques appropriate for the classroom. These techniques have required education personnel to sharpen their skills in systematically observing and analyzing ongoing patterns of reinforcement in the classroom.

In this context, the study of reinforcing behavior in the classroom provides one example of the role of systematic observation in helping us understand the classroom learning environment. Teachers' use of verbal approval and disapproval has been consistently observed to be effective in decreasing inappropriate pupil behaviors and in increasing desired pupil behaviors (O'Leary & O'Leary, 1972). The content of these approvals and disapprovals and the characteristics of the pupils to whom they are directed are important in understanding classroom life. One interesting procedure, the *Teacher Approval and Disapproval Observation Record* (TAD), developed by White, Beecher, Heller, and Waters (1973a) and White (1975), allows the observer to record teacher verbal approval and disapproval patterns as well as pupil variables and the preceding pupil behaviors to which the teacher had reacted.

Using the TAD, Waters (1973) studied sex differences in verbal approval and disapproval rates among teachers in first, second, and third grades. She found that there were no differences in the rates of approval given to boys and girls, but that boys received significantly more disapproval. Taking ability level into account, Heller and White (1975) observed the rates of approval and disapproval of junior high school teachers of social studies and mathematics who taught both "higher ability" and "lower ability" classes. Higher rates of disapproval were emitted in the lower ability classes and were predominately managerial in nature. More disapproval occurred in social studies classes than in mathematics classes. In all classes, little praise was given for appropriate social behaviors. Beecher (1973), studying teacher verbal approval and disapproval patterns in prekindergarten, kindergarten, and first-grade classrooms, observed different approval patterns at each grade level, but similar disapproval patterns across these grades. Observation studies such as these are of importance in understanding the existing reinforcement practices of teachers, given the potency of reinforcement in the classroom.

For readers interested in pursuing this topic further, the bibliography of this book includes selected observation schedules and accompanying guides for implementing behavior management techniques in classroom settings.

Observation and Psychoeducational Assessment

Pupil learning is an area of particular concern to most educators. In their daily interaction with pupils, teachers are continually assessing the degree to which desired learning goals are being reached. Indeed, observation is an integral component of this assessment process.

Certainly, systematic observation of a child's behavior can be an important tool for diagnostic assessment and case study in educational settings (Bersoff, 1973; Keller, 1986). Almy and Genishi (1981), in *Ways of Studying Children*, and Cohen, Stern, and Balaban (1983), in *Observing and Recording the Behavior of Young Children*, have pointed to observation as an integral component in assessing the learning needs of young children.

As an adjunct to standardized psychoeducational testing, gathering observations of a child within various natural contexts (home, school, playground) can generate rich developmental information regarding the child's current methods for coping with day-to-day situations, as well as his or her problem-solving strategies for particular tasks (Keogh, 1972). In collaboration with the classroom teacher, the school social worker, psychologist, and counselor can observe the child's interactions with peers in the classroom and other settings, and on another level, can view the ways in which the child relates to adults. Implicit in this process is the comparison of each child's performance with those behavioral norms concerning children of a similar age and background developed by the observer over time and as provided through sources such as normative data, individual measures of intelligence, and Piagetian tasks.

Within the testing situation, the school psychologist, learning disabilities specialist, and teacher can observe the gestures, actions, and other nonverbal behaviors that often contribute meaningful assessment data to the written test protocols. (See Alessi & Kay, 1983; Baker & Tyne, 1980; Lynch, 1977; Sitko, Fink, & Gillespie, 1977). Behavioral evidence is provided regarding the child's ease in relating to the tasks during assessment, rapport with the examiner, and general interest in the tasks. During individual testing behavioral information gained through purposeful observation might also include:

- Time taken to complete tasks.
- Approach of child to tasks—e.g., does child attempt difficult items or give up?
- Speed and accuracy of response—i.e., does child respond:

    Immediately and accurately?
    Immediately and then change answers?
    Immediately and does not consider alternatives?
    Slowly, but accurately?

- Amount of encouragement required—e.g., does child keep asking if he or she is doing well?
- Activity level of child—i.e., does child:

    Stay in seat with little movement?
    Stay in seat with repeated shifting around?
    Get out of seat occasionally?
    Get out of seat repeatedly?

- Amount of spontaneous talking child does.
- Physical features of the child (such as whether or not child wears glasses).

During group testing the observer can record such things as:

- Time taken by various children to complete task.
- Those children who have difficulty with presented instructions or in keeping their place.
- Which children skip difficult items, spend all their time on a few items, seem to be marking answers randomly, or repeatedly look around the room.

Interest in studying children's problem-solving strategies and intellectual styles has encouraged the observation of behavior in classrooms and test situations that reflect these strategies and styles (Bruner, Goodnow, & Austin, 1956; Ginsburg, 1987; Kagan & Kogan, 1970; Keogh, 1972; Kogan, 1983). These observations can help the assessor in matching psychoeducational interventions to the particular educational needs of a child.

Observation techniques are also useful in assessing the particular needs of children with special educational requirements. For example, observing the behavior of a hearing-impaired child or physically disabled pupil who has been placed in a "mainstream" classroom can provide ongoing data regarding the child's adjustment and the appropriateness of the educational placement. Several investigators highlight the use of observation strategies to improve the educational experiences of exceptional children (Gitler & Gordon, 1979; Kaufman, Agard, & Semmel, 1985; and Semmel, 1975).

Also, the assessment of adaptive behavior among institutionalized and noninstitutionalized mentally retarded, emotionally maladjusted, and developmentally disabled children has been dependent upon the use of reliable rating scales and behavioral checklists such as the AAMD (American Association on Mental Deficiency) Adaptive Behavior Scale—Public School Version; the Vineland Social Maturity Scale; and the Preschool Behavior Questionnaire (see Sattler, 1982).

Determining the optimal teaching techniques or interventions for children with special learning problems, in reading for instance, can often be accomplished efficiently by informal diagnostic procedures that include direct observation of the children's oral and silent reading behavior, in addition to traditional reading comprehension tests (Spache & Spache, 1973). The observant classroom teacher can recognize children who display symptoms suggestive of reading disability, and can provide these data as a basis for referral to other professionals for remedial programming.

Thus, while continuing to use tests or other appropriate strategies, the assessor should also use techniques of objective observation to raise and then confirm or reject hypotheses about an individual's functioning. Those engaged in psychoeducational assessment should seek naturalistic behavioral data to support their inferences. In fact, Public Law 94-142, the Education for All Handicapped Children Act of 1975, establishing safeguards for the evaluation and psychoeducational placement of children, has mandated the use of systematic, naturalistic observation techniques as complements to standardized testing practices (Heller, Holzman, & Messick, 1982). Furthermore, in determining the effectiveness of various intervention or remediation approaches, the school professional, needing to base conclusions on observable changes in behavior, has increasingly drawn upon naturalistic observation data to document the impact of the intervention program (e.g., Bissell, 1973).

Observation and Criterion-Referenced Assessment

The use of systematic observation techniques is particularly crucial in facilitating a "match" between a child's current level of functioning and the educational experiences to which he or she is exposed (Bloom, Hastings, & Madaus, 1971). Observations can provide an input to help formulate goals and select appropriate teaching procedures for working with a specific child. To provide a curricular match for the individual pupil, the classroom teacher must routinely assess whether a particular learning skill is being demonstrated and at what level (Boehm, 1973). Criterion-referenced testing is one form of assessment specifically related to the problem of the match. The question posed by this form of assessment is "To what extent is each pupil proficient in attaining the goal or goals of an instructional unit?" The criterion-referenced test, by definition, must be related to the objectives of an instructional unit. In turn, these instructional objectives must be stated in behavioral terms and broken down into their component parts. An additional consideration may be the variety of contexts in which learning is to take place. Thus, criterion-referenced assessment focuses on what the individual child can or cannot do relative to a given objective.

Systematic observation is frequently essential to the development and use of criterion-referenced tests. For example, if an educational objective is to evaluate self-help skills as they develop in young children, it would be necessary to define what is meant by "self-help" skills, consider which self-help skills would be of concern and when and in what contexts they might be demonstrated, and evaluate the individual child's progress by creating and using an observation procedure.

The criterion-referenced test may be contrasted with the more widely used norm-referenced test, which addresses itself to the issues of differentiating pupil achievement and making predictions. Although both forms of assessment are useful in educational settings, the distinction in purpose is critical. The criterion-referenced test evaluates a child's performance as it approximates specified lesson objectives, while the norm-referenced test compares the score of one child with the scores of others. Some useful resources in this area include Gagné (1985), Glaser and Nitko (1971), Gronlund (1985), Martuza (1977), and Popham (1971).

Observing the Effectiveness of Curriculum and Teaching Practices

Within classrooms, systematic observation has been used to generate information regarding the nature and effectiveness of varying instructional strategies (e.g., Good & Brophy, 1984). This book is not intended to present an in-depth exploration of these strategies, but some areas of application of systematic observation in studying the effectiveness of classroom practices may be of interest to the reader.

Flanders (1975) provided a framework for analyzing classroom interactions by observing teacher and pupil verbal behavior. Interaction analysis activities have provided the basis for pre- and in-service education programs that help teachers develop and control their specific teaching behaviors. The popularity of the Flanders Interaction Analysis model has been reflected in a burgeoning research literature in teacher effectiveness that has focused on discovering relationships between teacher behavior and measures of pupil growth (Good & Brophy, 1984; Joyce & Weil, 1972; Stallings, 1977).

With this understanding of the vital role that observational methods can play in the study of children, the educational process, and learning settings, let us begin to unravel the complexities of the observation process and to develop the skills necessary for systematic observation in early learning settings.

The Forms of Observation

There is a diverse range of written forms that our observations in learning environments can take, from informal, qualitative descriptions, to quantitative recording formats. These forms of observation include *diary descriptions, anecdotes, specimen records, checklists, rating scales,* and *observational schedules.* We will briefly describe these alternative modes of observing, highlighting their uses and limitations.

DIARY DESCRIPTIONS

Maintaining diary accounts of changes in human growth, behavior, and developmental events or milestones is the oldest observational method (Wright, 1960). Diary descriptions of young children's development have been kept by relatives, caretakers, and other observers close to the children. Diary entries are recorded in a narrative style and may vary from brief daily entries to comprehensive detailed accounts. The careful documentation of children's development in natural contexts can provide a strong data base for formulating hypotheses about human development, which in turn can be investigated through other methods of inquiry (laboratory experiments, field studies, and so forth).

The lack of reliability and unsystematic nature of these descriptions are potential problems. Another drawback is that diary accounts are almost always limited to one subject, or at best, a few subjects, making interpretations and generalizations difficult. Nevertheless, regular diary descriptions do provide a record of the continuity of behavior over time and can help one to identify meaningful patterns in development. Numerous independent diary descriptions, for example, of children's language acquisition, can lead to an increased objective understanding of typical developmental and universal norms.

ANECDOTAL RECORDS

Observers can write brief anecdotal summaries of their observations in any situation. These can range from developmental milestones — "Michael took his first step today" — to behavioral events —

"Mary was enthusiastic about her work on the microcomputer." Although anecdotes can be objective descriptions of events, they can also be subjective statements about these events. Many of us can recall "comments" sections on school records, which often included anecdotal observations such as "has difficulty relating" or "a pleasure to have in class." These comments were passed from one teacher to the next. In the past, unfavorable records could follow a child throughout his or her school career, perhaps biasing a new teacher's views of the pupil. Currently, many states prohibit the inclusion of such anecdotal accounts in official school records.

When they are factual accounts, anecdotal records can provide rich descriptive information related to child development. Anecdotal records can be made by teachers, child care workers, parents, or physicians, often at irregular intervals, to maintain a "factual" record. Anecdotes may or may not include what led up to or followed a recorded incident such as a temper tantrum. The choice of events to be recorded, timeliness of the record, and amount of detail provided are determined by the observer, who can choose to document unusual or unexpected events. Anecdotal records often reflect the biases of the observer. A number of procedures have been suggested for preparing and interpreting anecdotal records (Cartwright & Cartwright, 1984; Thorndike & Hagen, 1977). These include techniques such as:

- Limiting discussion to one incident
- Recording incidents as soon as possible after they occur
- Separating interpretive comments from factual reporting
- Considering supportive information

Clearly, although anecdotes can provide an understanding of behaviors not easily appraised by other means—such as social skills, adjustments, and health status—it is critical that objective, factual reporting take place and that follow-up study be made of behaviors of concern. Consideration needs also to be paid to how typical or representative noted behaviors are for the individual and for his or her peers.

SPECIMEN RECORDS

Specimen records are closely related to diary descriptions but represent the "continuous observing and narrative recording of a behavior sequence under chosen conditions of time and life setting" (Wright, 1960, p. 83). Observers detail the setting and record everything they see or hear. Thus behavior is described in its natural context. The resulting record is then reviewed and analyzed. Specimen records are useful to note small changes in development or behavior. A classic example is provided in *One Boy's Day* (Barker & Wright, 1951), a record of "what a seven-year-old boy did and of what his home and school and neighborhood and town did to him from the time he awoke one morning until he went to sleep that night" (p. 1). Eight observers, all familiar adults to the child, took turns during the day recording all directly observable behaviors, including vocalizations and body movements. They also recorded their own impressions. The extensive information gathered was later analyzed and a categorization of behaviors and identification of behavior sequences made.

Specimen records provide comprehensive accounts of behavior and are useful for establishing the range and types of behaviors a person may exhibit in a given situation. They may serve as a basis for formulating observational questions and developing structured observational procedures, and can be used for detailed analyses and quantitative study. Although extremely valuable, specimen records are especially time consuming and costly. The use of audiotapes or videotapes could enhance the reliability and completeness of this form of observation.

Within the classroom, the teacher can engage in a brief form of continuous observation, generally referred to as a *running record*. For example, the teacher may choose to maintain a running record of everything a child does and says during an assigned activity (see the example below). Five minutes of such recording may result in important insights.

A SAMPLE RUNNING RECORD

Subject: Tom
Setting: Second-grade classroom; 31 students
Situation: Class members were to work independently on a reading assignment that included a reading passage followed by five questions
Observation time: 10 minutes
Observer: Judith Zucker

Tom held a looseleaf in his lap. His reader was opened to the appropriate page on his desk. His desk was cluttered with other books and pencils.

T. wrote for approximately two minutes. He copied questions from the board, seemingly looking at the board after writing each word of a particular question. He completed the copying of only one question by the end of the two-minute span.

T. stopped writing and began to play with a tape dispenser that was in his desk. He tore off pieces of tape and pasted them on the inside of his desk. During this time he spoke to himself using the phrases: "Oh boy," when he tore off an exceptionally long piece of tape; "Just one more piece," after which he did stop tearing; "What's the next question?," looking at the board but not copying; and "Ick!" During the time T. looked at the board, he held a small piece of tape between his thumb and forefinger and moved his forefinger toward and away from the tape.

He began to write again. (I reminded the class to answer questions in complete sentences.) T. grimaced. He began to search inside his desk for a pencil. He found one, examined it, rejected it, found another pencil with an eraser. T. spent roughly two minutes erasing all of what was written on his paper thus far. He brushed away the eraser remains. He stated, not too quietly, "Uh oh! My paper ripped."

T. attempted to repair the paper with tape. He tore off a piece of tape. He made an unhappy face—apparently the piece of tape was too small. He started to tear off a second piece but lost the end of the roll of tape. He put his hand to his head. He tried to find the end of the tape again. He struggled with the tape for almost a minute, scraping the roll with his fingernail.

Defeated, he tore a sheet of paper out of the looseleaf and elaborately crumpled it. He placed the looseleaf on his desk slowly, put his head down, placed two hands on the desk, and pushed himself away from the desk. He stood, extending his arms to both sides, stretched, looked at me, and walked slowly to the wastebasket carrying the paper. He threw the paper in basket, walked to my desk, and said, "Miss Z., my paper is ripped."

T. returned to his seat. He began to look for a pencil and clean paper. He repositioned the looseleaf and reader as before. He began to write his name on the paper.

This approach allows the observer to focus his or her attention on one individual and provides an opportunity to become acutely aware of behaviors of the student that may have previously gone undetected. A limitation of this approach is that it is virtually impossible to record all of a subject's behaviors, due to one's inability to write fast enough. Furthermore, while the observer is writing, the subject is continuing to "perform," and these actions go unnoticed. The use of audiotape or videotape, although solving some of these problems, introduces others (see Unit X).

CHECKLISTS

Checklists involve a listing of behaviors that are marked by the observer as being present or absent; other behaviors are ignored. Sometimes checklists are used to track behaviors of interest on several occasions or in different settings. (Checklists usually are *sign systems*, a topic discussed on page 58). Checklists may be completed while actually observing the child, but are more frequently completed "after the fact" from memory.

Checklists can help child care workers or teachers understand a variety of behaviors such as self-help or study skills. In order to develop a useful checklist, behaviors must be clearly defined and listed beforehand — the usefulness of the checklist depends on whether or not it includes all possible key behaviors (Fewell, 1984). In order to generate this list a *task analysis* needs to be carried out that requires the developer to ask, for example, "What does the child need to be able to do to demonstrate good study skills?" "How, specifically, might these behaviors be demonstrated?" Many areas of complex behavior, such as peer relationships or task-appropriate behavior, can be analyzed through this approach. Thus, checklists can reflect a teacher's behavioral objectives and can help focus the observer. Several checklists in fact can be used concurrently.

Unfortunately, not all checklists are well detailed or task analyzed. The user needs to review the use of a potential checklist carefully to consider the adequacy of the information yielded. Other problems relate to such issues as bias and selectivity. Checklists can reflect a particular theoretical perspective and provide a biased view of the observational situation. Finally, checklists provide no information regarding the degree or frequency with which a behavior is exhibited. Those checklists that provide space for narrative elaboration can help users evaluate the extent or degree to which the observed behaviors are exhibited.

RATING SCALES

Rating scales focus on designated behaviors and allow observers to judge the extent or degree to which these behaviors are exhibited. Rating scales require judgment and are often used in the assessment of personality and social adjustment or physical motor development. Although ratings can be made while observing ongoing behavior, they frequently are made on the basis of past observations and are completed when the child is not present. Rating scales usually take one of two forms, numerical judgments or descriptive phrases (see Figure 3.1).

Information based on ratings can be useful for assessment purposes. An example may be found on the Pupil Response Sheet from the *Cognitive Skills Assessment Battery*, second edition (Boehm & Slater, 1981, p. 3) (see Figure 3.2). Other examples include *The Pupil Rating Scale* (Myklebust, 1971) and the *Developmental Task Analysis* (Valett, 1969).

Ratings tell us nothing about the causes of behaviors, but they can help us to describe or pinpoint specific behaviors. The observer must make a judgment about the most descriptive behavior or provide a numerical rating. Bias can influence judgment, particularly when numerical scores are solely used or where the target behaviors are not directly observable and therefore require inferences to be drawn by the observer. Caution also needs to be exercised with scales that provide a midpoint score, such as:

$$1 \quad 2 \quad 3 \quad 4 \quad 5$$

always   never

When using these kinds of scales, there is a tendency for observers to rate at the midpoint and to avoid extreme judgments (error of central tendency).

Kerlinger (1973) has suggested that rating scales are particularly

Figure 3.1.   Forms of Rating Scales

a. Numerical judgments, from high to low, of behaviors of interest, such as:

Easily relates to classmates   1 2 3 4 5   Has difficulty relating to classmates

b. Descriptive phrases, such as:

Very attentive	Generally attentive	Often inattentive	Very inattentive

c. Specific qualities or objectives stated in terms of performance, such as:

Unable to print name	Prints first name only	Prints first name & last initial	Prints first & last name

Figure 3.2. Example of Ratings Used During Assessment

A: Task Persistence

4 ☐ persists with task
3 ☐ attempts task briefly
2 ☐ attempts task after much encouragement
1 ☐ refuses

B: Attention span

4 ☐ focuses attention voluntarily
3 ☐ attends with teacher direction
2 ☐ some distraction with noise or movement of others
1 ☐ easily distracted

C: Body movement

4 ☐ sits quietly
3 ☐ some squirming
2 ☐ much movement
1 ☐ out of seat; body constantly in motion

D: Attention to directions

4 ☐ listens carefully to entire direction
3 ☐ attends only to brief directions
2 ☐ plunges ahead after hearing only portion
1 ☐ plunges ahead immediately

E: Comprehension of directions

4 ☐ rapid comprehension of most directions, given age expectations
3 ☐ understands after several repetitions
2 ☐ partial comprehension of directions
1 ☐ does not appear to comprehend most directions

F: Verbalization

4 ☐ many spontaneous comments
3 ☐ occasional comments
2 ☐ responds only when spoken to
1 ☐ extremely reluctant to speak or inappropriate speech

G: Ease of relationship (rapport)

4 ☐ immediately friendly
3 ☐ friendly but reserved
2 ☐ shy
1 ☐ very reluctant and/or fearful

H: Confidence

4 ☐ very sure of self
3 ☐ confident with things known; attempts new things with encouragement
2 ☐ reluctant to try new or difficult things
1 ☐ very uncertain; needs much encouragement

Source: Boehm and Slater (1981), Cognitive Skills Assessment Battery, second edition.

susceptible to a number of sources of bias including the "halo effect," error of severity, error of leniency, and the error of central tendency (see Unit VII). Kerlinger has also pointed out that the "Halo is extremely difficult to avoid. It seems to be particularly strong in traits that are not clearly defined, not easily observable, and that are morally important" (p. 549).

Rating scales, however, have the advantages of being easy to use and applicable to a wide variety of situations. They can help focus an observer's attention, particularly when points along the scale are behaviorally defined: The more observable and precise each point, the greater the objectivity of the results. The advantages of rating scales and their ease of use leads to two cautions. First, it is essential that ratings be based on a sufficient number of observations to arrive at a valid judgment. Second, observers need to be mindful that many rating scales do not specify precise behaviors and should be aware of their own sensitivities and biases in making ratings.

FORMAL OBSERVATION SCHEDULES

Observational systems are developed to help observers collect and quantify information using systematic procedures and recording schedules. Use of such procedures helps make the information gained from observation more manageable. Useful observation systems include:

- Category or sign systems that clearly define target behaviors and are exhaustive of the behaviors to be observed
- Procedures for sampling behavior, such as time or event sampling
- Standard recording formats
- Procedures for determining reliability

Users tally or mark the occurrence of or frequency with which behaviors occur in predetermined categories during each observation unit, such as every 30 seconds or every minute. If categories are exhaustive, nonoverlapping, and well defined (see pages 54–55) and if recording procedures are well defined, formal observation systems can be efficient and reliable, and can enhance the quantification of observational data. The development of such observational systems is the major focus of this text.

The use of formal observational systems does not eliminate all problems. Since the use of formal schedules focuses the observer's attention on targeted behaviors or events, observers may miss other important behaviors or may not be able to capture the flow of behavior. Also, the amount of training required to use many systems may be extensive. Despite these limitations, observational systems can provide sophisticated and valid accounts of a wide range of observable behaviors. (Useful resources regarding observational systems may be found in the Bibliography.)

There is a place for each of the forms of observation in learning settings. Often more than one mode of observing can be used, in a complementary manner. For example, a specimen record, rating scale, and formal observational schedule might be successively employed over time in addressing a particular observational problem. Flexibility in using the array of observational techniques can be the hallmark of the skillful early childhood observer.

The Selective Nature of Our Observations

Each person presented with the task of making specific observations should be able to observe objectively with minimal interference from subjective frames of reference. Obviously, however, the subjective is always going to be a factor — we each choose to pay attention to certain things or activities while we ignore others. It is impossible to observe everything in a given situation at the same time; while we are focusing on some attributes of a situation, we are naturally missing others.

To help you become acquainted with your own current approach to observing situations, try this task.

TASK 1: OBSERVATIONS OF YOUR PRESENT SETTING

Observe the setting in which you find yourself. Record your observations, using the Task 1 Worksheet. If others are in the room with you, ask them to engage in the same task. Record your observations in the order in which they are made. Limit the time for the task to five minutes.

Then compare your observations with those made by others in the same setting. Include in this comparison:

The observations made (what you and others selected to observe)

In what sequence your observations were made and how the sequence of your observations compares with that of others

And then consider these questions:

How did you choose what to view?

Did you employ a strategy for observing the setting? If so, which strategy?

How did the format of the task influence the nature of your observations?

TASK 1 WORKSHEET

Observations of Your Present Setting

(Five-Minute Time Limit)

Setting: _____

Time of Day: _____

Observer: _____

Observations in Sequence

  1.

  2.

  3.

  4.

  5.

  6.

  7.

  8.

  9.

10.

11.

12.

Given in the Appendix is a set of sample responses made by three observers in the same setting. Compare your responses with these.

Although it is interesting to note the similarity in responses among the three observers as they viewed the same setting, this example illustrates the selective nature of observing a setting, both in terms of what is observed and the order in which the observations are made.

SUBJECTIVITY IN OBSERVATION

By now it has become apparent that a wide range of observations are possible, given the same setting and time, depending upon the selectivity of the viewer. The selective and *subjective* nature of what we see is a reflection of many psychological factors, such as previous observation in that setting, our attitudinal framework, our momentary feelings and mood, and any systems of classification we may have for viewing the world, which can be an indication of our interests and occupation.

For example, when an early childhood specialist observes the child of a family friend playing with a puzzle, the child's behaviors are likely to be compared with known developmental milestones gained through reading and past experiences.

TASK 2: OBSERVATIONS OF A SUPERMARKET SCENE

For Task 2, view the photograph of a supermarket scene and make your observations, attempting to take the points of view of the manager of the store and then of a shopper. Again, limit yourself to five minutes for each observation. Record your observations on the Task 2 Worksheet.

Next, compare the content and order in which the observations were made given the two different orientations. Consider: (1) in what ways they are the same and how they are different, and (2) why you think these differences have occurred.

Certainly, the differing orientations of the store manager and shopper for observing the supermarket will influence the kinds of observations that are made. The manager, interested in the level of business and the related satisfaction of customers, would focus on the number of shoppers, the number and nature of items in shopping carts, the orderliness of the shelves, counters, and aisles, as well as other indications of the efficiency of staff. On the other hand, the shopper would probably focus observations on the cost and kinds of items available. As is the manager, but for other reasons, the shopper would be interested in the cleanliness of the store, the orderliness of the aisles, the apparent freshness of produce, and so on. Our needs and points of view influence what we see.

Some other questions that could be posed giving focus to observation in supermarkets include: What products do

Task 2. A Supermarket Scene

people buy? How many customers use shopping lists? How many customers (any individual entering the store) are in the store at various time periods?

AIMING FOR OBJECTIVITY IN OUR OBSERVATIONS

Tasks 1 and 2 demonstrate the *selective* nature of our perceptions. Such selectivity is natural because the process of perception demands selectivity. When we are observing in order to make decisions or to draw conclusions, it is necessary to be *objective*, to have a focus so that our observations are purposeful and defined. Therefore, we must consider

TASK 2 WORKSHEET

Observations of a Supermarket Scene

Observations in Sequence

Manager of Store

1.

2.

3.

4.

5.

6.

7.

8.

9.

Shopper in Store

1.

2.

3.

4.

5.

6.

7.

8.

9.

such questions as: "What are we going to view?" and "For what purpose?" Such questions increase the objectivity of the observations that we make. The following guidelines are given to help you differentiate objective from subjective observations.

- Objective observations (factors or details others could readily agree upon):

    A count of the number of chairs, tables, windows, and so forth, in a room
    Noting the color of objects
    Relating the size of objects one to another
    Describing behavior as it occurs (but not interpreting this behavior)

- Subjective observations (unique perceptions, biases, or individual points of view that others might not agree with):

    A statement about perceived conditions, such as "This room is hot" (it may not seem hot to others)
    Focusing on the physical attractiveness of a room
    Concentrating on personal characteristics of the people in the setting, such as "She looks pretty"

It is possible to carry the quest for objectivity to the point of absurdity: "The walls of the room are painted light yellow, shade #428 ACME Opaque paint and the air temperature in the room is 72.4°F." Under most conditions, this degree of precision would, of course, be unnecessary.

TASK 3: DISTINGUISHING OBJECTIVE FROM SUBJECTIVE OR INTERPRETIVE OBSERVATIONS

Go back to the record of observations you made for Task 1 and consider which of your reactions conveyed *specific* and *objective* information, and which ones involved subjective observations, employing the guidelines just given. Label each of your observations "objective" or "subjective" in the margin of your worksheet.

If your observations tended to fall heavily in the subjective category, you have an indication of one's natural tendency to view situations subjectively. There is nothing wrong with making subjective comments so long as the observer is aware of the subjectivity and that this is reflected in the use of qualified language: "The air *feels* cold" not "The air *is* cold."

An additional dilemma that faces the observer is the tendency to make inferences or draw conclusions from scanty evidence not necessarily supported by other data. Thus, if you noted that a girl sitting to your left appeared to be happy and what you actually saw was a girl with a smile on her face, you might be drawing an inappropriate conclusion on the basis of the evidence—the smile might hide disdain, discomfort, or boredom.

THE EFFECT OF THE OBSERVER'S PRESENCE

Look at the pictures of a classroom in Figures 4.1 and 4.2. They illustrate the effect of an outside observer's presence, in this case with a camera, on the spontaneous flow of behavior in a given setting. The first photograph was taken immediately upon the observer's entrance into

Figure 4.1. School Classroom

Figure 4.2. Classroom after Photographer Enters

the classroom; Figure 4.2 was taken several seconds later while the observer (with camera) stood by the doorway of the room. In Figure 4.2 the child in the striped shirt has responded to the observer. This illustrates how the presence of a photographer, or any observer, can influence the nature of some behaviors that occur as part of the ongoing sequence within that setting.

However, it has been noted that, in general, the effect of the presence of the outside observer on pupil behavior tends to decrease over time (Masling & Stern, 1969). With this in mind, it is important to note that the observer, if he or she is new to a setting, should be within that setting on several occasions prior to making systematic observations or drawing conclusions based on those observations.

DRAWING INFERENCES

Until now our emphasis has been on objective observing. However, such an emphasis is not intended to negate the importance of drawing inferences as a result of the observation process. Inferences can generate ideas, hypotheses to be checked out against other evidence, and also, potentially creative solutions to problems. Thus, inferences about another person's feelings ("Linda appears to be a happy child," or "Michael seems to be a bright, well-adjusted child"), supported by a variety of observational data such as facial expressions and the content of conversations over a period of time, can lead to certain conclusions made or actions taken in the classroom, on the job, at home, or in relationships with others.

Though we will not move into a philosophical discussion here, it is essential that we now consider the nature of various inferences that are commonly made in education settings. Each day educators make statements such as:

> Louise is a creative child.
> Johnny isn't very bright.
> The boys in this room are hostile and aggressive.
> Jerry is not distractible and attends well during class.
> Irene has a very poor self-concept.

Psychological phenomena such as creativity, intelligence, aggressiveness, distractibility, and self-concept are not directly observable. Rather, these labels or descriptions are used or made on the basis of observable behaviors that represent commonly agreed upon indicators of the constructs just noted.

Although all of us make inferences about others each day, few of us are aware of the way observations provide support for such inferences. Taking the example of "self-concept," what do we mean when we refer to a child's good or poor self-concept? We need to raise such questions as: What observational data can be used to support the inferences and conclusions drawn? Would another person arrive at the same conclusions? How many instances of particular observable behaviors are necessary before we are willing to state that a child has a poor self-concept? (Sampling and the systematic collection of observational data to lend support to inferences are topics dealt with at length in Unit VIII.)

Let's consider the role of observations in making inferences with the following example.

TASK 4: OBSERVATIONS OF A GIRL IN A NURSERY CLASS

For Task 4, look at the photograph of a girl in a nursery school and consider what objective statements could be made about her and what inferences might be drawn about her behavior in the context of the activity and classroom.

Task 4.   Girl in Nursery School Setting

The following information will help clarify the situation:

The girl and the other children are four years old and have attended nursery school for two months.

The children are engaged in free play, which generally continues for about 30 minutes.

The girl has been sitting in the same place without making any sounds for at least five minutes.

Using the Task 4 Worksheet, indicate possible inferences about the girl's behavior in the classroom, supporting your statements with objective observational data. Indicate by corresponding letters which observations are the basis for your inferences.

Review your list of inferences about the little girl in the picture and their supportive observations. Then consider the possible observations and inferences for Task 4 given in the Appendix.

TASK 4 WORKSHEET

Observations of a Girl in a Nursery Class

Observations Made	Inferences Drawn	Observations Supporting Inferences (#1, #2)
1.	A.	A.
2.	B.	B.
3.	C.	C.
4.	D.	D.
5.	E.	E.

In making observations and inferences in most situations we have the benefit of viewing the flux of behavior over time. A single photograph obviously presents a static moment in time, making it essential that the viewer question what actually preceded that momentary instance. Prior to the situation depicted in the picture shown in Task 4, the girl might have been actively involved in play with the boys in the block area, or she might have just sat down after playing with a group of children in the dollhouse area. If the viewer cannot obtain such information about prior activities, care should be exercised about drawing strong inferences. The strength of inferences depends on the prevalence or the frequency of the observed behavior that supports the inference. Sampling behavior over time eliminates the tendency to draw inferences on the basis of scanty observational data.

Defining the Problem
and Describing the Setting

By now it should be apparent that making useful and objective observations is a complex task. The classification or organization of behaviors and components of the setting can facilitate the objective observations process, as well as the communication of findings to others. The type of grouping or classification used must relate to the particular focus or concern of the observer. For example, a kindergarten teacher interested in developing appropriate concept materials for a class would focus on a child's use of the particular concepts to be developed, while ignoring the child's social interaction with others. On the other hand, if the teacher wanted to develop a program that encouraged social interaction among children, care would be centered upon a concern with ways of classifying social patterns in the classroom.

In this unit we seek to develop a systematic approach to structuring observations so that enough data can be gathered to realize the goals for which observation techniques were used in the first place. Given the inherent selectivity in the observation process, and the need for objectivity discussed earlier, agreement between individuals on the specific foci of observation is essential. Although ways by which the reliability of observation can be increased will be considered in the next three units, it becomes essential at this point to develop an approach that can do the following:

- Force the observer to clearly define the problem or question he or she wishes to answer through the use of observation techniques.
- Take into account the constraints a given setting imposes on the scope of potential behaviors, and lead the observer to describe the components of an observational situation, including the overall physical setting, materials available to individuals within the setting, and individuals within the situation.
- Provide a system for describing, counting, and categorizing instances of behavior, allowing more than one observer to collect or interpret the same data.

• Take into account the position that one cannot directly observe emotions, cognition, or attitudes. Rather, the latter are concepts that are inferred on the basis of viewing countable, describable instances of behavior.

DEFINING THE PROBLEM

The range of questions that might be posed in learning settings and for which observation techniques are appropriate is broad. A curriculum coordinator might be intent on evaluating the influence a new social studies curriculum has on questioning behaviors displayed in the classroom; teachers or psychologists in training might want an overview of the range of typical behaviors exhibited by children from different age groups attending the same school; the school psychologist posed with a referral of a child demonstrating "learning difficulties" might be interested in that child's classroom behavior as he interacts with his peers, teacher, and the learning situation; a principal of a large urban school might want to know if pupils receive more feedback on assignments when student teachers are present.

Some sample problems that provide focus for the classroom observer follow.

The teacher might be interested in the number of activities involving more than one child that occur during the school day. The teacher might be interested in this observation in order to make inferences about the "cooperative behavior" of children in the classroom.

The teacher, concerned about the performance of John Jones, and questioning the appropriateness of a referral to the school psychologist, might want to know if John appears to understand curriculum content, is smaller than other children in the classroom, is very quiet, is inattentive, or does not respond to classroom instructions or directions.

The principal, concerned about lack of space in the school, might wonder if the class makes effective use of space currently allotted.

The supervisory teacher might be concerned by the extent to which a student teacher is providing practice appropriate to specific goals of the lesson.

Posing questions or presenting problems in a form that allows the observer to understand the specific purpose of the intended observations and eventually arrive at an answer to the posed question is essential. For example, the question "Are the pupils in this class motivated to do their assignments?" in its current form is insufficiently defined to focus the observer on specific behaviors in the setting, because one must ask:

What is motivation?
Can motivation be observed directly?
What, in specific behavioral terms, is "doing" an assignment?

If the question is rephrased to read, "Do pupils in this class regularly (over a stated time period) turn in completed class and homework assignments" it limits the observer to directly observable behavior — turning in a completed assignment — and does not deal with motivation, which can be inferred only from a variety of observed behaviors.

TASK 5: DIFFERENTIATING CLEARLY STATED FROM POORLY STATED QUESTIONS

As a further exercise, determine which of the questions given on the Task 5 worksheet are clearly stated. Check the appropriate column for each question and fill in the reason for your response. When you have completed this task, compare your answers with the judgments about each question given in the Appendix.

THE CONSTRAINTS OF THE SETTING

After defining the problem for observation, a careful analysis of the setting itself is needed in order to develop appropriate categories for observation. The general setting characteristically dictates the nature of behaviors that can be observed in that situation; for example, a child's verbal interactions with adults cannot be observed if that setting is restricted to children. It is also important to focus on those aspects of the setting that can limit, direct, or facilitate behavior. These factors include:

- People in the setting who will differ along the dimensions of age, sex, and role
- Tangible materials in the setting
- General physical characteristics of the setting itself such as temperature, lighting, room size, and space

TASK 5 WORKSHEET

Differentiating Clearly Stated from Poorly Stated Questions

Question	Well Stated	Poorly Stated	Reason
1. Are boys more restless than girls during small-group reading-readiness activities?			
2. Does the teacher in this classroom encourage questioning behavior?			
3. During a given kindergarten class day, how many individual children choose to look at a book during free play?			
4. Why do the girls in the kindergarten class appear to be more motivated to clean up after snack time?			

An overview of the total setting is helpful in developing an understanding of the situation, but it is also important to reemphasize the selective nature of observing behavior. An individual will ignore those portions of a setting where little activity is occurring and will focus on areas of the setting where the central activity is taking place.

The constraints of a setting on the behavior of an individual can be illustrated from another perspective. For example,

How does the same child interact with others in the classroom, in the gym, on the playground, and at home?

How does the factory worker interact with other workers during rest periods, in the cafeteria, and on the job itself?

Roger Barker (1968) made a useful point in his exposition of the mutual relationship that takes place between people and their environment. The environment, or *context* of behavior, has its own structures (boundaries, and physical and temporal attributes), that limit or dictate the individual's behavior. A child's behavior on the playground is different from that in the classroom; on the playground the child is more likely to run and shout than in the classroom. A doctor generally functions differently on the golf course than in a hospital; on the golf course the doctor's behavior resembles that of other golfers, while in the hospital it is like that of other doctors. Clearly, the setting makes a great difference in the doctor's behavior. Thus, the interaction that takes place between an individual and the setting generates an important question: What characterizes the behavior of the same person in different situations or settings?*

Pursuing this point further, particularly with younger children, we might consider a child's behavior separately in different activity areas of the room, such as in the doll corner, at work tables, in the block area, at the book shelf, or in the painting area. With older pupils, we might consider behaviors as displayed in different subject matter classrooms or curricular periods. In summary, then, the observer needs to take into account the various constraints within settings that limit or provide opportunity for the behaviors of individuals within those settings.

TASK 6: CONSTRAINTS IMPOSED BY THE SETTING

Considering our analysis of constraints on possible behavior imposed by the setting, look at the photograph of a playground setting. Using the Task 6 Worksheet, list those characteristics of the people within this setting that might restrict behavior. Speculate on some possible behaviors that

*Barker and Wright's *One Boy's Day* (1951) provides stimulating reading in this area.

Task 6. A Playground Setting

probably could not occur because of these constraints and on some behaviors that would be facilitated by these same factors. Also consider in what ways the available "materials" (play equipment, play space) on the playground tend to produce some general constraints and in what ways they facilitate certain kinds of behavior.

Compare your responses with the sample responses given in the Appendix.

ANALYZING THE COMPONENTS OF THE SETTING

Further considerations in viewing the contexts in which one observes behavior are components such as the physical setting, tangible materials of the setting, and individuals within the setting. These components are described individually in the following section, and practice in observing them is given in the accompanying tasks.

Observing and Describing the Overall Physical Setting

Unlike human behavior, which undergoes considerable change over time, the physical setting in which we observe behavior usually remains quite stable. When observing, one should consider the physical charac-

TASK 6 WORKSHEET

Constraints Imposed by the Setting

Category	Characteristics	Unlikely Behaviors	Likely Behaviors
1. People			
2. Materials			
3. Space			
4. Other (Indicate)			

teristics of the situation, such as the temperature of a room and its implications for the kinds of behavior to be expected in that room, the amount of space provided in the setting for a range of activities, and the nature of artificial and natural lighting and its placement within a setting.

Observing and Describing Tangible Materials

Tangible materials might be considered next because they are often central to the behavioral activities in a setting. Such materials include large pieces of equipment (desks, playground equipment, sandbox) as well as smaller, more easily expendable materials (paper, pencils, books, puzzles, and teacher-designed materials).

Aside from identifying and describing these materials in isolation, it is important to note the arrangement or organization of these materials by people within the setting to meet their particular goals. For example, the larger setting might be organized into activity areas, such as seat activities, library corner, science area, or arts and crafts area (as illustrated in the photograph shown in Figure 5.1).

Figure 5.1. Kindergarten Classroom

Observing and Describing Individuals Within the Setting

A third major component of our analysis of the setting in which behaviors are observed is a description of the individuals within that setting. Task 7 provides practice in doing this.

TASK 7: VISIBLE CHARACTERISTICS OF INDIVIDUALS

Look at the Task 7 photographs and write down your descriptions of the *visible* characteristics of each individual pictured, using the Task 7 Worksheet. As you will notice, the Task 7 Worksheet lists only characteristics that are *directly observable*. In making descriptions of individuals, one should not feel compelled to make inferences about the emotions, social backgrounds, current roles, and so on, of these individuals. To do so would be an example of how often we draw conclusions and make judgments about individuals based on characteristics that are beyond what we actually can see.*

An observer interested in a subset of children (such as a reading group), or only one child, has more flexibility for description than would be possible in a larger group. Obviously, in a classroom group of 20 children, it is impossible for the observer to focus careful attention on more than one child at a time. Therefore, if the observer is interested in describing the physical characteristics of an entire group of children, it is necessary to employ a technique that allows for systematic ordering of observations of the group, viewing one member of the group at a time.

It is important to emphasize that we are observing individuals at this point without considering their behavior and without considering the ways in which they interact with each other, physically or verbally. After describing the individuals whose behavior is of interest to you, it is helpful to take notice of some general characteristics of the group of people within the setting. Such *summarizing characteristics* include:

The number of individuals present
The ratio of boys to girls
The ratio of adults to children

---

*Kleinmuntz (1967) offers a detailed discussion of observing expressive behavior (pp. 92–109).

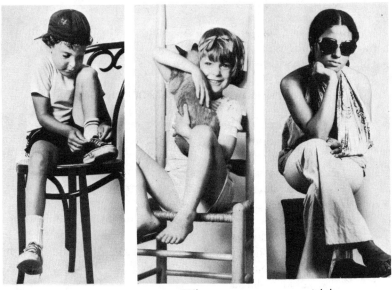

Boy   Girl   Adult

Task 7.   Three Individuals

THE CONTEXT OF BEHAVIOR

In this unit we have isolated the various key components of a setting that need to be considered when observing. In an attempt to illustrate the ways in which physical features of the setting, the objects and the people within that setting, combine to produce the context of observed behavior, consider the example given in Figure 5.2. Here we are observing in the library of an elementary school. The time is the library period for second-grade pupils. For this observation, we have taken note of the physical features of the room, the objects in it, the people and their activities, and we have included a list of summarizing characteristics.

As Figure 5.2 shows, the observed activity is a result of the interplay of people with their setting, in this case a school library. Now do Task 8, using the example in Figure 5.2 as a model. Pick a similar setting.

TASK 8: KEY COMPONENTS OF A SETTING

Analyze the components of a setting. Distinguish physical features, objects, and people, and name the activities taking place. Write your responses on the Task 8 Worksheet.

TASK 7 WORKSHEET

Visible Characteristics of Individuals

Category	Boy	Girl	Adult
1. Approximate Age			
2. Sex			
3. Physical Features Shade of hair, clothing, body build, height, glasses			
4. Movement and Gestures			
5. Physical Handicaps			

Figure 5.2. Key Components of a Setting

Setting: Elementary-school library
Time: Library period for second-grade pupils

Physical Features	Objects	People	Activities
Rectangular room	Three rows of steel bookshelves outside	One young girl in blue dress	Copying a drawing from a magazine
Entrance and exit turnstile	One wooden bookshelf against the wall		
Yellow colored walls			
One large glass window	Two yellow and one green chair with a small table in one corner	One middle-aged woman in green dress	Often coming out from the adjoining room with a paper in hand
One small glass window			
Two pillars	Six round tables, "natural wood," each with five chairs		Checks the paper with the girl
One adjoining room with a window door	Index card boxes		Goes back to her room
One big door leading into library	Books on the counter	Two young boys in the rows of bookshelves	Searching for books
	Books in the shelves		
Check out counter	Duplicating machine	Three young girls sitting at one of the round tables	Two girls talking with each other while pointing to a picture in a book; one girl looking at book in front of her
Overhead fluorescent light turned on	Painting of a man		
	Three plants		
	Paper slips, pins, stamps on the counter		
	Bulletin board		

Summarizing Characteristics

—Presence of only six students in the library suggests that only small groups of second-grade pupils use the library at a time, not the entire class, because, at the time of the observation, only the six students were there, although there was ample room for a class.

—Turnstile present for counting or control.

—All individuals present seem occupied.

TASK 8 WORKSHEET

Key Components of a Setting

Setting:
Time:

Physical Features	Objects	People	Activities

Summarizing Characteristics:

Summarize the characteristics of the setting and activities that take place. Then, focusing on the constraints imposed by the setting, make predictions about which kinds of behavior are likely to occur. Do you find that these predictions more or less correspond to the observed activities?

We have stressed the importance of observing and describing the environmental contexts in which classroom behaviors occur in order to generate an awareness of the constraining influences.

In describing environments, it is important to remember that the classroom is constantly changing—another adult can enter the room, class groupings change with the curriculum, a particular child is absent, and so forth. Since behavior is always determined to some extent by the environment in which it occurs, it is sometimes important to describe the shifts within the environment.

It should be emphasized that the study of environment *per se* and the relationship between individuals and their settings has been a central focus of the field of ecological psychology (as discussed in Unit II). A complex network of theoretical constructs, empirical findings, and field methods has resulted from the ecologist's perspective. The purpose of this unit has been no more than to highlight some components of a complex study of "behavior settings" that can be useful to the early childhood observer.

Labeling and Categorizing Behavior

The term "behavior" has been used earlier in the book, but we have not defined it precisely because our focus has been on other aspects of the complex observation process. In order to consider dimensions for labeling behavior, let us define "behavior" as *any observable, overt action or activity that an individual exhibits in a setting.* Behaviors range from solitary, nonvocal activity (sitting in a chair, looking out the window) to verbal and nonverbal interaction with others (a fist fight and verbal exchange between two third-graders on the playground). When referring to constructs such as "self-concept," which we cannot directly observe, we are dealing with an inference or conclusion that may be based on observable behaviors.

DIMENSIONS FOR LABELING BEHAVIORS

Within education and the behavioral sciences one can select from a variety of measures, rating scales, and categories for viewing behavior in the classroom (see Bibliography). Recently, the variety of efforts to measure behavior have reflected a behavioral analysis orientation. The resulting instruments have focused on the teacher's verbal behavior as well as on a wide range of verbal and nonverbal pupil responses, and have in general been devised in a manner consistent with purposes of the particular researchers. Although we advocate a perspective that places behavior within the context of its setting and that underscores the importance of making qualitative judgments, inferences, and decisions on the basis of observation data, we also advocate an approach that allows us to consider behavior from various points of view. Consequently, a cognitive-developmental psychologist might make inferences about the level of a child's cognitive-intellectual functioning on the basis of observing behaviors defined as related to cognitive functioning. On the other hand, an early childhood educator might make inferences about the age-appropriateness of certain social behaviors as a result of observing children interact in a kindergarten situation. Furthermore, inferences about a child's emotional maturity and level of affective expression might be drawn from observing behaviors that theoretically are considered attributes of a given emotion. Our approach allows the observer, whatever his or her philosophical stance or professional role, to employ direct observation for the kind of analyses and interventions that he or she feels are most appropriate.

Despite the dogmatism of many developers of observation techniques, it is important to remember that observation systems differ in the extent to which they can be applied or generalized to situations other than those for which they were designed or developed (Kerlinger, 1973). Therefore, it becomes the burden of every observer, having defined his or her purpose, to determine the appropriateness of a particular observation system or series of behavioral categories. To help the reader evaluate a particular system, we will raise a number of issues that should be considered in evaluating observation systems and in deciding which approach to use for sampling behavior.

Knowing and Defining Behaviors

Since most observation systems are designed for particular research purposes, the developers of these systems focus on those behaviors related to the objectives of their particular project. For example:

- A researcher interested in observing a teacher's questioning behavior should consider all the types of questioning behavior that are conceivable in classrooms.
- A teacher interested in observing the "hyperactivity" of a particular child needs some understanding of behaviors that are representative of "hyperactivity."

Thus, observing human behavior requires some knowledge of that behavior (Kerlinger, 1973). It would not be possible for a novice to observe systematically a doctor's operating room behavior without some understanding of the procedures employed. From this knowledge base it becomes possible to list potential categories for observation.

In their overview of various observation systems, Simon and Boyer employed a major distinction between affective and cognitive observational systems. The individual interested in studying the classroom's emotional climate and "how it [the classroom] is conditioned by teacher reactions to pupils' feeling, ideas, work efforts, or actions" (Simon & Boyer, 1967, p. viii) would use an affective system. If, however, the individual were more concerned with studying verbal patterns in the classroom or in children's problem-solving techniques, a cognitive system would be more appropriate. *Mirrors for Behavior: An Anthology of Classroom Observation Instruments* (Simon & Boyer, 1967, 1970, 1974) provides a more detailed characterization of these two generalized category systems, with examples of different classroom observation systems.

Once the observer has defined the problem or question, the observations must be structured so that they can be:

- Communicated in an organized fashion to another individual who was not present
- Generated in a manner similar to another observer viewing the same behaviors at the same time

MUTUALLY EXCLUSIVE AND EXHAUSTIVE CATEGORIES

Mutually Exclusive Categories

In order to eliminate confusion as to which observed behaviors are to be recorded in which categories, and to increase reliability (see Unit VII), it is essential that clear definitions of behavior be indicated so that each category of observable behavior is precisely distinguishable and independent from other categories (is mutually exclusive). "Asking a question" and "making a statement" are mutually exclusive categories, for a person can engage in only one of these behaviors at the same point in time. Other examples of mutually exclusive categories are standing and sitting, driving and swimming.

If the observer has difficulty deciding whether an observed behavior belongs in one category rather than another because of overlapping definitions of those categories, the classifications are not mutually exclusive and need refinement. For example, "Using correct grammar" and "asking a question" are not mutually exclusive categories. In this example, if a pupil asks a question and the question is grammatically correct, the observer would have difficulty categorizing that observation.*

---

*On another count, from the point of view of clear definition, the first of these categories would need to be specified so that observers would know what is meant by "grammatically correct."

Task 9 provides practice in distinguishing examples of mutually exclusive categories.

TASK 9: DISTINGUISHING MUTUALLY EXCLUSIVE CATEGORIES

In the examples given on the Task 9 Worksheet, indicate whether the clusters of categories are mutually exclusive or overlapping. Then check your responses in the Appendix.

Setting Limits

As the observer defines the basic problem or area of interest for observing, it is necessary to set limits on the universe of behaviors to be observed. For example, an individual interested in studying "teaching behavior in the classroom" must delimit a problem area to provide focus, such as studying types of teacher questions, categorizing teacher statements, or counting the number of approvals by teachers to pupil responses. If the observer chose to focus on types of teacher questions, all other behaviors would be ignored and the observer would attend only to questioning behavior — that is, the universe of behavior. Furthermore, if the observer were interested in studying teacher questioning behavior in the classroom, the categories would have to subsume the total range of possible behaviors that constitute teacher questioning behavior. For example, the teacher asks for:

Specific fact
Definition
Opinion
Clarification or elaboration
Application
Evaluation

Making Categories Exhaustive

The categories must be exhaustive in that every instance of observed questioning behavior (or every behavior in the universe being considered) can be classified in one of the available categories. As Kerlinger (1973) has noted, the universe of behaviors that the observer considers can vary in scope depending upon the objectives of the observation process or question being asked. Task 10 provides practice in establishing exhaustive categories.

TASK 9   WORKSHEET

Categories	Mutually Exclusive	Overlapping
1. running lying prone sitting in place standing in place		
2. laughing crying talking		
3. reading looking listening		
4. asking a question giving a command stating an opinion		

TASK 10: ESTABLISHING EXHAUSTIVE CATEGORIES

Develop an exhaustive series of categories for the following defined universe of behavior:

Large-muscle coordination (gross motor skills) as exhibited by four- to six-year-olds during playground activities.

In developing your list of categories, you should consider the following questions:

What is an operational definition of large-muscle coordination?
Is the problem as stated precise enough to avoid considering behaviors other than "large-muscle coordination" as observed on the playground?

List the categories on the Task 10 Worksheet.
As you may have noticed, there is some degree of ambiguity as to what constitutes large-muscle coordination. Therefore, you might have asked for a clearer definition, such as "a child exhibiting behavior on the playground requiring use of the legs, arms, head, and/or body." By excluding manipulation with hands, fingers, and toes, we eliminate fine motor skills from the definition.

TASK 10   WORKSHEET

Categories of Large-Muscle Coordination Playground Activity

1.	6.
2.	7.
3.	8.
4.	9.
5.	10.

As you might see when comparing your list of categories with that of the sample responses given in the Appendix, an independent observer employing your list of categories might observe a behavior that could not be categorized on your list. Therefore, employing an "other" category in the development of your observation schedule allows the list of categories to be refined at a later observation session. For example, in using the list presented as a sample response, how would a child's activity on a teeter-totter be classified? This would need to be classified in the "other" category because there is no other appropriate category. If the "other" list began to have a large number of tallies, it would be necessary to refine the original listing to be more comprehensive.

SPECIFYING CATEGORIES

In devising categories and defining behaviors one also needs to consider the specificity of what one actually observes. It must be determined whether very narrow, easily observed, specific behavior units or broader chunks of behavior are going to be employed. For example, considering displays of affective behavior in the classroom, one could note the number of times a child smiles during an hour or the number of grimaces in a given time period. Instead an observer could more broadly categorize affective behavior in terms of the percentage of time a child spent in interactive play. The broader category "interactive play" encompasses a wide range of discrete behaviors.

When individual observers employ a system of narrowly defined categories, their consistency and agreement in classifying behaviors is likely to be high. By reducing the behaviors to be observed to such detail the observer also greatly reduces the degree of inference introduced into the observation processes, eliminating subjectivity to a greater extent than when broader, more global categories are employed. However, if the behavioral units become too discrete—finger tapping or counts of eyeblinks—the observer may have difficulty making generalizations or "abstracting" from these observations, and the observations can become meaningless data for the teacher though they might not be for an experimental psychologist.

When categories are narrow ⟶ observer agreement is high ⟶ the degree of inference is low ⟶ generalizations are more difficult to make ⟶ subjectivity is low.

On the other hand, if very broad categories are used, more difficulty is encountered in achieving agreement between observers. Using the category "anxious behavior" versus "nonanxious behavior," the lack of specificity allows much leeway for subjective interpretations of the meaning of these categories. Is a twitching foot classified as an example of "anxious behavior?" Broader categories that lack definition or specificity require the observer to make more subjective interpretations of observed behavior before classifying an observation into a given category. Although reliability is decreased by employing broader categories, the observer may be making a more meaningful and useful interpretation of the problem at hand.

When categories are broad ⟶ observer agreement is low ⟶ the degree of inference is high ⟶ generalizations are easier to come by ⟶ subjectivity is high.

The learner of observation skills should aim at a minimum degree of inference: categories that are too vague allow different observers to place different interpretations on the same behavior; categories that are too specific, although they cut down ambiguity and unreliability, are often too rigid and inflexible for easy application.

CATEGORY AND SIGN SYSTEMS

From another perspective, Medley and Mitzel (1963) discuss two approaches to the construction of items for an observation schedule. The first approach, called a "category system" requires the observer to list a set of categories such that every observed behavior can be recorded into one, and only one, of a series of mutually exclusive categories. The categories within this system must also be exhaustive for a particular dimension so that every observed behavior can be categorized. For example, Flanders (1965; 1975) devised a schedule listing 10 types of verbal behavior that might conceivably occur in the classroom. Using Flanders' system, every utterance of the teacher or pupil can be classified.

As another example, we can make our own list of mutually exhaustive categories for a particular situation. If we were to investigate the nature of interactive play at the preschool level, we would list mutually exclusive and exhaustive categories of interaction. On a recording format similar to the Category System Sample Worksheet (Figure 6.1), one could list the categories, using as many columns as necessary for the number of children being observed. The sample given is an observation of interactive play among preschool children.

The observer using such a system records and *categorizes* every behavior that each individual child demonstrates. The record of observations for a given time period shows the total number of units of behavior observed and their frequency classified into each category for each child and over the entire group sampled.

In contrast, a "sign system" involves listing beforehand a limited number of specific kinds of behavior of interest to the observer. During a stated observation time period the record of observations will show which of these behaviors actually occurred and which did not occur. An observer using a sign system approach records only those behaviors that fall into one of the preconceived categories listed. Presumably, many behaviors would not be recorded at all and would be ignored. Therefore a sign system includes mutually exclusive categories, but the categories do not need to be exhaustive.

For example, one might be interested in observing rule-following behaviors using a sign system. The Sign System Sample Worksheet (Figure 6.2) gives an observation of students' ability to follow some selected class rules. In using the sign system in this example, the observer has determined the behaviors that indicate following class rules. Using a similar worksheet, the observer would record instances of the students demonstrating these behaviors. The observer would use as many rows as

Figure 6.1. Category System Sample Worksheet

Interactive Play

Category	Child A	Child B	Child C
Solitary play			
Parallel play			
Interactive play with one child			
Interactive play with more than one child			
Interaction with adult			
Looking around only			

Figure 6.2. Sign System Sample Worksheet

Following Selected Class Rules

Child	Remains in Seat	Raises Hand	Talks in Turn

necessary for the number of children and as many columns as necessary for the number of behaviors.

Note that here there are no "other" or "etc." categories. Behaviors other than those in a given category would be ignored because they are irrelevant to the purpose of the observation.

In summary, the major distinctions between category and sign systems could be characterized as follows:

Category System	*Sign System*
Every observed behavior must be classified	Only *specific* predetermined behaviors classified
(Exclusive *and* exhaustive categories)	(Exclusive, *but not* exhaustive categories)

DEVELOPING CATEGORIES

A number of steps might be taken to develop categories that are appropriate to the observational task at hand:

1. *Brainstorming.* Think through all possible approaches to your problem. For example, "Is my observational question clear and specific?" "Can it be answered through observation?" "Are the behaviors I've chosen to observe relevant to my question?"

    Brainstorm the problem with your associates. How do they perceive the behaviors you wish to target? Discuss areas of agreement or differences. This discussion can help lead you to the categories you employ in your observational instrument.

2. *Reviewing.* Survey the literature. How have others approached the same or similar problems? Are their definitions of the target areas complete? What procedures have been used, and what were the outcomes? What stumbling blocks were encountered?

3. *Task-analyzing.* Break down the behavior to be observed into its component parts — engage in a "*task analysis*" (see Gagné, 1985). Ask what subbehaviors or events make up the targeted domain of behavior. For example, in order to develop categories of verbal communication among preschoolers, one would generate a list of the kinds of verbal behaviors that are possible and would exclude nonverbal behaviors:

    Asking for assistance
    Seeking information (asking a question)

Commanding
Mimicking
Making statements of fact, hope, and so forth

4. *Previewing.* Go into a situation that is representative of the setting in which you will need to observe and generate a running record or describe carefully those behaviors of interest. Consider whether or not the observation was typical, representative, and adequate. From these observations, hone into your question and abstract the important behaviors or events (see also Martin, 1976).

One could pursue any or all of these activities depending on the difficulty of the categorizing task, previous experience, and one's patience!

Making Reliable Observations: Avoiding Observational Bias

OBTAINING RELIABLE OBSERVATIONS

To help both teachers and behavioral scientists working in education to draw the conclusions necessary for making daily decisions and solving problems, there must be agreement on the observational bases for these conclusions or inferences. Precise, unambiguous specifications of what behavioral activities are to be focused upon are prerequisite to structuring or organizing behavioral observations. Such precision in defining an observed behavior increases the extent to which various observers report similarly about the behavior on which they have focused.

Given: Definition of purpose of the observation
A specific point in time
Aim: What you see = What I see

Observer Reliability

The greater the agreement between two independent observers, the greater the consistency or "reliability" of both viewers. For example, if teacher A and teacher B are both observing Jimmy, a seven-year-old second grader, during reading group, their observations are likely to differ if they do not share a clear definition of what behaviors they should focus on. They are not likely to draw a consistent conclusion about Jimmy's attention to reading materials if they have not focused on the same attentive behaviors at the same point in time.

Furthermore, precise definitions force individual observers to be consistent with themselves. The more precise the definition, the less the opportunity for subjectivity to be introduced into the observation process.* For example, if teacher A wants to count the number of times preschoolers in a defined setting display "dependency" behavior, the teacher will have difficulty consistently labeling specific behaviors as "dependent" unless he or she has made a careful listing of "dependent" behaviors before observing. Generally, the more specific and complete these criteria for labeling behaviors, the more consistent the observer will be in pinpointing behaviors over time (see Figure 7.1).

Many readers of the educational and behavioral science literature will discover reports on the inter-rater reliability for a particular observation instrument. These statements of agreement among observers in recording observations are generally indicated in the form of reliability coefficients, which range from the point of no agreement (0) to perfect observer agreement (+ 1.0). Generally one tends to find reliability coefficients reported in the range of + .70 to + .95. As the coefficient approaches + 1.0, the reliability increases, and we have more confidence in reliable observations among observers.

Observer Agreement

The rate of agreement between two or more observers working at the same time may be determined as shown in Figure 7.2. Observers should aim for rates of agreement of .80 or better. Note that we have no check here as to whether the same behavior instances were observed, but only the rate of agreement between observers. If, however, we employed a time-sampling system (see Unit VIII), by which each observer records only one behavior during each observational interval (that is, every five seconds), we could also determine whether or not the same behaviors were being observed.

Figure 7.1.   Observer Reliability

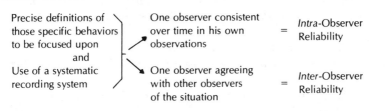

*More detailed discussions on the various types of reliability may be found in Foster and Cone, 1986; Hartmann, 1982; Hollenbeck, 1978; and Kent and Foster, 1977.

Figure 7.2. Determining Rate of Agreement Between Observers

Steps	Example: Teacher questioning patterns in a seventh-grade social studies class		
1. Count the number of instances in each category for observers A and B.	Category	Observer A	Observer B
	Teacher asks for:		
	Specific fact	ᵀᴴᴸ //	ᵀᴴᴸ
	Opinion	////	///
	Application	/	//
2. Total the number of observations for A and B.	Total	12 +	10=22
3. Count the number of agreements in each category and over categories for both observers.	Agreements:		
	Specific fact		5
	Opinion		3
	Application		1
	Total		9
4. Divide the number of agreements by the total number of observations.		$\frac{9}{22}$ =	.409
5. Multiply the quotient by the number of observers—in this example there are two.		2 x .409 =	.82
	Rate of Agreement	=	.82

Once an observer has determined his or her rate of agreement with another observer, the decision may be made to follow the same procedures without the second observer being present. It is, therefore, periodically useful for observers to spot-check their rates of agreement in order to assure accuracy.

Another procedure for assessing observer agreement is in fact to consider instances where *behavior does not occur* (Hartmann, 1982; Vasta, 1979). In the same situation, two observers can:

- Agree that a behavior occurred
- Disagree, in that observer 1 indicates a behavior occurred, while observer 2 does not
- Disagree, in that observer 2 indicates a behavior occurred, while observer 1 does not
- Agree that a behavior did *not* occur

Thus, one can evaluate the rate of agreement for occurring and nonoccurring behavior or events. Baker and Tyne (1980) have suggested that the use of the formula for observer agreement described in Figure 7.2 can overestimate agreement when behaviors or events occur with high frequency. In contrast, observation of infrequent behaviors or events can result in lower reliabilities. In such cases, one might also consider intervals when only one observer notes the behavior or when both agree that behaviors did not occur.

Stability of Observations

Observer agreement, although essential, is insufficient to assess the reliability of one's observational system. Repeated visits need to be made to a setting in order to establish the stability of observations. For example, if one were concerned about a group of students completing their math assignments, it would be necessary to observe these students over time to determine if a consistent pattern of behavior were exhibited. If "aggressive" behavior was exhibited by two pupils, the teacher might question if this were a chance occurrence. The teacher would need to observe the pupils over time. By correlating the observational outcomes for two or more occasions, a *stability coefficient* can be obtained (see Foster & Cone, 1986; Kent & Foster, 1977; and Rowley, 1976, 1978; for detailed descriptions of calculating stability measures).

In establishing the stability of observations, one raises the practical question of "how many observations are required in order to have confidence in the findings?" Clearly, there is no one correct answer for this question — the number of observations needed and the schedule for observing is tied to the observer's purpose.

Consider these different observation questions and the frequency of observations required in order to produce stable, reliable observation outcomes.

1. How do the spatial concepts "top" and "bottom" develop in preschool three- and four-year-old children?

   • Repeat observations of the same children over time; for example, once per month for a year.
   • Alternatively, observe a number of subjects at different age levels performing the same tasks.

2. What pattern of peer interactions does Jesse display?

   • Observe Jesse a minimum of three times in situations where peer interaction is possible.

3. Does a behavioral intervention improve Mary's on-task behavior in mathematics?

- Observe Mary during mathematics for five minutes each day for one week prior to the intervention (baseline).
- Next, observe Mary for five minutes each day in mathematics during the intervention.
- After an appropriate time period, try removing the intervention and record Mary's behavior daily.
- Return to the intervention, if necessary, to maintain improved behavior and continue to collect observational data daily.

When conducting psychoeducational research using observational techniques, one will often demand a greater number of observations in order to draw conclusions than when arriving at daily decisions in the classroom. In the research context, one will also more likely observe in a range of different situations, classrooms, or schools, before confidently generalizing about the effects of an intervention, the impact of a teaching strategy, or the value of a curricular innovation.

Rowley (1978) has reviewed some interesting work by John Herbert and associates at the Ontario Institute for Studies in Education that helps set guidelines for collecting observational data. Each of 30 teachers was observed for 50 minutes on six to seven occasions, using the "System for Analyzing Lessons." Rowley focused on how the reliability of observational data is affected by (1) the number of observation periods, (2) the length of the observation period, and (3) the combination of varying the number and length of observation periods. Three major conclusions were drawn:

1. Reliability increased with more frequent observation periods.
2. Although reliability increased with the length of the observation period, the greatest increment occurred when the observation period was increased from 10 to 20 minutes. After 20 minutes, the reliability leveled off.
3. The optimal combination of number and length of observation periods was five periods of 30 minutes each ($r = .705$).

However, the implications of this work for the classroom observer with limited time and resources are to make three observations of 30 minutes duration or to arrange four observational periods of 20 minutes duration.

The length of these observational periods could be accommodated by typical class schedules.

CHALLENGES TO RELIABLE OBSERVATIONS

Unfortunately, gathering reliable observational data is not an automatic, common-sense, "anyone can do it" activity. There are many sources of error that can creep into the process, distorting the validity of the conclusions based on the data. An extensive literature documents different sources of error or bias (e.g., Baker & Tyne, 1980; Fassnacht, 1982; Kazdin, 1982; Kent & Foster, 1977; Taplin & Reid, 1973). Error can derive from the *observer*, the *observee*, and the *observation instrument*. Each of these potential sources of bias will be highlighted, and possible solutions to the problems suggested.

Observer Bias

Perhaps the most significant sources of error are observers themselves.

Personal bias or expectation. Let's consider an example involving Janie, a pleasant and cooperative six-year-old. She hands in her homework on time, and the teacher likes her and expects her to do well. A new girl joins the class and is being teased by some of the other girls. The teacher, wanting to get at the source of the problem, observes and records "teasing" behavior in the classroom. Although Janie makes faces at the newcomer, the teacher overlooks this behavior. Bias has occurred due to the teacher's beliefs and expectations about Janie. When such bias is positive, placing the observee in a favorable light, it is called a "halo effect"; when the bias is negative, it might be called "prejudice." Thus, prior experiences between the observer and observee can influence the outcomes of observation (Kazdin, 1982).

Systematic training can help the observer increase objectivity by facilitating awareness of one's personal biases. Since each of us has different tolerance levels or thresholds for different situations, we need to be attuned to our attitudes about such distracting behaviors as an individual's "good" manners, quick response styles, or repetitive question-asking. A "violent outburst" of anger to one observer might be seen as "within normal limits" by another (Good & Brophy, 1984).

Potential biases associated with an observer's sex, race, age, and cultural or ethnic identity must all be addressed in the particular observational setting. Finally, the theoretical perspective of the viewer (Freudian, Piagetian, Rogerian, or whatever) can certainly affect or color what one sees and how it is perceived.

One needs to have an accurate perception of potential sources of personal bias.

Knowledge of hypotheses.   In pursuing observational research, it has been widely demonstrated that observers who know the purpose of the study or the hypotheses being tested will more likely record observations that tend to support the hypotheses. Therefore, to correct such potential biases, most research designs include observers who are "blind" as to the purposes of the study.

In classroom life, however, such controls are not always feasible. However, a colleague of the observer (another teacher, school psychologist, or other school professional) might observe in a targeted classroom, unaware of the specific problem or the particular child who is experiencing a problem (Baker & Tyne, 1980).

Observer drift.   Observers often use instruments or procedures that require extensive pretraining to achieve observer agreement. Once in the field, after having employed the instrument for a length of time, the observer will frequently begin to "drift" when recording observations, becoming less precise and less accurate. Drift of another type might also occur: Observers who always work together will tend to agree ("consensual drift"); their observations will become more alike over time (Hartmann, 1982). When possible, the use of regular unannounced reliability spot-checks to monitor an observer's accuracy is warranted. This might be accomplished by having two observers in the setting during a selected sample of sessions. When a large number of observations are gathered, approximately 10 to 20 percent of the total should be checked; with a small number of observations, a minimum of two checks should be made.

Inadequate training.   The most inexcusable source of behavior error is poor training. Many observation systems need to be practiced extensively before being used in a classroom setting. Adequate time needs to be planned for practicing, feedback, and guided discussion. The practice might take many forms, such as use of videotapes or team observing. A criterion level of 90 percent agreement with an expert observer's ratings should be achieved prior to employing an observation instrument. Observers need to know and practice the rules and procedures of any observational system they use. See Boice (1983) for detailed suggestions on improving observational skills.

Observee Bias

Changes in the observee.   The teacher observing in his or her own classroom is known to the pupils and is expected to be observing them. Consequently, students are not as likely to alter their behavior in the teacher's presence. (Certainly, if a forbidden activity is being pursued and the teacher approaches the scene, children will change their behavior quickly!)

Individuals also modify some of their behavior when an outside observer enters the setting and when they know they are being observed. This change in behavior is generally referred to as "reactivity."

Knowledge of being observed. If individuals know they are being observed, and particularly if they know why, they might behave in ways to please the observer, such as remaining in their seats, raising their hands more often, or asking more questions. Other individuals become more nervous and display signs of anxiety not normally shown.

Ethics, of course, dictate that individuals who do not belong in a particular setting must receive permission (from observees or their parents) to observe in classrooms, testing rooms, or other settings. It is not easy to hide the fact of being observed from even the youngest child.

Despite these obstacles, steps might be taken to reduce observee reactivity:

1. The observer can visit the classroom or other setting several times, so that students become accustomed to his or her presence. Usually one or two visits is sufficient for younger children. Older children might need more visits to become acclimated; early observations may need to be discarded.
2. Participant observers such as other teachers, paraprofessionals, and older students might be employed and be less obtrusive than strangers (Baker & Tyne, 1980).
3. Observation rooms with one-way mirrors might alleviate reactivity more quickly, but one cannot observe classroom settings this way. Also, if observees turn their backs to a one-way mirror, many behaviors are not seen.

Intrusiveness of equipment. The use of video recordings or tape recordings (see Unit X for more detailed discussion), although solving some of the problems that arise from an observer's presence, can be intrusive. The equipment must be introduced to the setting, not unlike introducing a human observer.

When we videotaped preschool classrooms, for example, we set up the equipment a day ahead of time and used the opportunity for trial runs. The children soon adapted to the cameras, cables, and equipment operators. The activities of the day quickly became more interesting than the video intruders. The one significant distractor was a microphone that reminded some children of a gun; a quick modification was made.

The Observation System as a Source of Errors

Two issues need to be considered to minimize possible errors due to the observation system: the match of the system and the complexity of the system.

Match of the system.   When observers in classrooms select from available observation instruments, they need to consider if an instrument effectively matches their observational purposes. Are the behaviors targeted by the selected instrument appropriate to address the questions raised by the observer? The issue is paramount as well when observers develop their own instrument. This match refers to the validity of the observational measure, a topic discussed in Unit VIII.

Complexity of the observational procedures.   The more complex an observational system, the greater the opportunity for error. Those systems that require many decisions on the part of the observer, involve complex categories, or demand memorization of many codes, are more vulnerable to error. The use of clear, precise observational questions and simple, nonoverlapping coding categories reduces the possibility of such error.

Our discussion of the sources of observational error has highlighted some of the threats to reliable observational data. Accounting for reliability is essential if one is to have confidence in observational techniques. A brief checklist, presented in Figure 7.3, summarizes the critical issues discussed in this unit.

Figure 7.3.   Summary Checklist for Making Reliable Observations

Issue	Considerations
1. Objectivity	Specific behaviors listed beforehand
	Eliminating bias due to personal
	belief or expectation
	Not knowing the hypotheses
2. Clear, usable recording format	Nonoverlapping categories
	Avoiding complex coding systems
3. Inter-observer agreement	Aiming for 90% or better
	Adequate training
4. Avoiding observer drift	Systematic spot-checks
	Two observers present 10–20% of time

Sampling and Recording Behavior

WHAT'S TO BE OBSERVED

Once an observer has selected appropriate categories of behavior on which to focus (Unit VI) and in order to maximize reliable observing (Unit VII), it is necessary to devise a plan for systematically sampling observations in the setting. The approach is the same as that of the microbiologist who wants to determine the purity of water in a lake for drinking purposes but who, for obvious reasons, cannot test the whole lake. She draws test samples from many parts of the lake so that her total sample will be representative of the lake as a whole. Moreover, she draws samples at different times, so that they will be representative over an extended period of time. In the same manner, it is unfair to judge the effectiveness of a comprehensive in-service training program on the basis of an observation of only one teacher at one point of time during the year.

One issue facing the observer confronting the myriad of behaviors that occur over time is the procedure for selecting specific behaviors for observation. For example, the observer may opt to record all behaviors during the school day of a given child (generally referred to as a diary description or running record). However, while observing this one child, the behaviors of the other children, perhaps engaged in similar activities, will be missed. Therefore, it is vital for the observer to decide ahead of time the sampling procedure to be employed. Two useful sampling procedures, time sampling and event sampling, have been detailed by Herbert Wright (1960) and are described in the next two sections.

Time Sampling

According to Wright the observer using a time-sampling procedure attends to the occurrence or nonoccurrence of selected behavior(s) within specified, uniform time limits. "The length, spacing and number of intervals are intended to secure representative time samples of the target phenomena. As a rule . . . descriptive categories are coded in advance for quick and precise judgements in the field and later efficient scoring" (1960, p. 93). Thus, the length, spacing, and number of time units are determined by the purpose of the observer.

An example of this would be the observer interested in the ability of second-grade students to remain on a specified learning task. He could check each of 25 students for 10 seconds every five minutes, throughout a given part of the science period, to see whether each was "off task" or not. A descriptive list of behaviors to be considered "off task" would have been made prior to the observation, and it would include such particulars as "looking around the room," "being out of the seat," and "engaged in unrelated activities." For another observer question, the appropriate sample interval might be every minute, or every 10 minutes, or every day of a week, or during other subject time periods.

One suitable worksheet format is given in Figure 8.1, Procedure A. Here, each child's off-task behavior would be recorded at each sample interval, using as many lines as necessary for the number of children being observed. Again note that a listing of off-task behaviors would have to be determined ahead of time.

It is important to use a simple form of coding or abbreviating that facilitates recording of the observed behaviors. Typically, in time sampling, behaviors are recorded within predetermined categories in the form of checkmarks or tallies. These marks or tallies yield information about *whether* a particular kind of behavior occurred (one checkmark) or *how often* it occurred (tally marks) during an observation period.

In Procedure A, where only one category is involved, no coding is required; a checkmark for any 10-second interval records an occurrence of off-task behavior. Using longer time intervals for each child, the observer might use tallies to record several discrete occurrences of a behavior in each interval.

Another observer, however, concerned with subcategories of off-task behavior, would develop a coding system for the specific behaviors. This is shown in Figure 8.1, Procedure B. In this example, the observer has determined this code:

L = Looking around (seated)
O = Out of seat
U = Unrelated activity (seated)

Off-task behavior would be indicated by a checkmark in the L, O, or U column; no mark would indicate on-task behavior. The observer would

Figure 8.1. Time Sampling

Procedure A
"Off Task" Behavior*

Child	Time Unit							Total
	10:00	10:05	10:10	10:15	10:20	10:25	10:30	

* Within each time unit observe each child for 10 seconds, record for 10 seconds, move on to the next child, and so forth.

Procedure B
"Off Task" Behavior (Pre-coded)

Child	10:00			10:05			10:10			10:15			10:20			10:25			10:30			Total		
	L	O	U	L	O	U	L	O	U	L	O	U	L	O	U	L	O	U	L	O	U	L	O	U

use as many lines as necessary for the number of children being observed.

It should be noted that exactly the same information recorded on the Procedure B worksheet could have been recorded on the uncoded Procedure A worksheet. Instead of simply making a checkmark for a given 10-second unit, the observer using Procedure A could write an L, O, or U, depending on which category of off-task behavior was observed. However, an advantage of having the categories precoded on the recording form is that it is much easier to make checkmarks under coded columns than to memorize and record the code. Another advantage is that when sampling is completed, the results are already tabulated.

The coding system (the categories and their codes) must always, of course, be memorized before sampling begins; moreover, the observer should always have an outline of the coding system at hand in case of memory lapses. Obviously a system can be most easily and reliably memorized if the codes are abbreviations or other symbols designed to remind the observer of the categories themselves. (As codes for the off-task behaviors categorized above, the letter abbreviations L, O, and U are easier to remember than the numbers 1, 2, and 3 would be.) And when such codes are present as tabulators on the record form, they constantly reinforce the observer's memory of the coding system.

Such helps are extremely valuable in time sampling. Remember that the observer must proceed from one preset time interval to the next, ready or not. The difficulty of using a memorized coding system is of course greatest when the time units are very small (the Flanders system requires the observer to record a code number every three seconds) and the number of categories relatively large. The procedure can be taxing, and its efficient use requires considerable practice.

The more detailed the coding system used, the fewer the number of individuals that can be observed in a given time interval. Thus, before observing, a balance needs to be arrived at between:

The most appropriate time unit
The number of individuals to be observed
The detail desired from the observation

Going back to the example of on-task behavior in a science class cited earlier, the observer could decide to observe only a sample of the 25 pupils present and obtain even more detailed observational data on each child.

Generally, time sampling is useful for observing behaviors that occur frequently and at a somewhat regular rate.

Event Sampling

Event sampling simply allows the observer to record a given event or category of events each time it naturally occurs. When the event occurs, the observer describes it and, if desired, describes the antecedents to that event. The range of events one might choose to record is practically limitless and, again depending upon one's purpose, might range from pupils' use of abusive language to demonstrations of independent study skills. The major advantage of event sampling is that it allows one to observe events as they naturally occur and in context. For example, a preschool or special education teacher might be interested in pupils' self-help skills, determining ahead of time to observe such skills as:

Going to the bathroom unassisted
Washing hands
Buttoning clothing
Putting on boots
Tying shoelaces

The teacher may observe and record for each child the date on which that child acquired these skills, or when these events occurred. A recording format such as the one presented in Figure 8.2 might be employed for these observations. The observer would use as many columns as necessary for the behaviors being observed, as many lines as necessary for the number of children, and would record the date on which the child demonstrates the skill.

Figure 8.2.   Event Sampling Procedure

Self-Help Skills

Child	Bathroom Unassisted	Washes Hands	Buttons Clothes	Puts on Boots	Ties Shoelaces

While maintaining a record such as this, the teacher can determine the frequency of the behavior for a specific child or group of children. (In a special education class, the categories might need to be broken down into finer units.)

An important outcome of time and event sampling is that two observers can simultaneously view and record the same events, permitting later determination of the extent of observer agreement or consistency in sampling and recording observations.

Time versus Event Sampling

In summary, time and event sampling each have distinct advantages and limitations, which are presented in Figure 8.3.

Many systems combine both time and event sampling. For example, the frequency and nature of events such as teacher praise are of interest to many educators. The Teacher Approval/Disapproval Classroom Record (TAD) (White et al., 1973a) views the rate of teacher verbal approvals and disapprovals during daily instruction. Taking into account when a class period starts and finishes, the observer notes the time at which each approving or disapproving teacher behavior occurs. The specific pupil behavior and teacher response are recorded along with pupil characteristics (Figure 8.4).

This system is interesting in that a recording interval of 20 seconds is employed whenever an approval or disapproval occurs. The total

Figure 8.3.   Time versus Event Sampling

Advantages	Limitations
TIME SAMPLING	
• Good agreement among observers. • Good reliability over time. • Good control over the mechanics of the system.	• The frequency with which the events of interest occur may not be represented accurately—e.g., events that occur frequently within a time unit may be underrepresented in total calculations if a ± system per time unit is used.
• Provides a good overview of the range of behaviors and events occurring in a particular setting.	• Infrequent events may not be represented accurately. • The duration of events is not assessed.
EVENT SAMPLING	
• Helpful in describing events of a particular kind that have been detailed before the observation takes place. • Every natural occurrence of the targeted behavior is sampled.	• Breaks up the natural continuity of behavior. • May not provide information as to what sets off a particular event.

Figure 8.4. Sample TAD Recording

Time Start	Activity	Time	Teacher Response	Pupil Behavior
9:17 A.M.	Reading group, 5 boys	1 hr. 45 min.	1. A ⓓ You're not telling me what it means	Incorrect answer to question
			2. Ⓐ D Right	Correct answer to question
End of class period 11:02 A.M.				

amount of recording time (the number of such intervals multiplied by 20 seconds) is subtracted from the total observation time, allowing the rate of actual observation to be calculated. (However, as with other systems, another approval or disapproval could occur during the recording time and not be included.) The results of 16 studies (in K–12) employing TAD (White, 1975) have shown that:

1. Teacher approval is highest in grades 1 and 2, after which it declines sharply, to 4 to 8 approvals during a class period.
2. Teacher disapproval also declines after the primary grades.
3. Teacher approvals occur more frequently than disapprovals in grades 1 and 2, but thereafter disapprovals occur more frequently than approvals.
4. Teacher approval rate is higher for ongoing instruction than for classroom management.
5. Teachers emit more approvals to pupils learning at a faster rate than to those working at a slower rate.

Thus, the usefulness of this time and event measure has been well documented.

In addition to time and event sampling, procedures are available to help observers evaluate behavior in ongoing situations. These include interval recording and accounting for duration.

Interval Recording and Accounting for Duration

Interval recording is another sampling procedure that is related to time and event sampling. Interval recording involves dividing the observation period into time intervals. Thus, a 30-minute class period might be divided into 10 intervals of three minutes each. Depending on the observation purpose and system, the observer using interval recording can detail:

- The occurrence or nonoccurrence of behaviors
- The frequency of target behaviors within each interval
- The duration of behavior within an interval
- The portion (beginning, middle, end) of the interval in which the behavior occurred.

Recording duration allows observers to report not only the frequency of behaviors but also the persistence of behavior over time. Thus, a teacher could observe exactly how long a child persisted with an activity or how much time a child was off task during an instructional period. (For more details see Alessi & Kaye, 1983, and Foster & Cone, 1986.)

Other Aspects of Sampling

Number of behavior categories used.   The number of behaviors an observer can take account of at one point in time is limited. According to Medley and Mitzel (1963, p. 330), "The number of categories into which the behaviors are to be coded should not be too large; few studies have used more than ten. It seems desirable to define the categories so that their average frequencies are roughly equal, but experience has shown that in some instances categories used less than 5% of the time function effectively." Use of more than 10 or 12 categories, however, makes serious demands on memory and requires extensive training.

Representativeness of the behavior sample.   In order to determine the representativeness of most behaviors, it is necessary to observe the occurrence of a given behavior at different times of the day and on different occasions. If a behavior happens only once or on rare occasions, it is not representative of overall behavior. Therefore, before making conclusions, it is important to assess the *frequency* of the behaviors.

Anecdotal records are a case in point. Records are often made of unusual behaviors ("He stole the money that was on my desk") or of only one form of behavior (more likely to be negative than positive): Unfortunately such information frequently follows an individual, even if it is not representative of that individual's overall functioning. In the final analysis, anecdotal information cannot be given much weight unless a record of the frequency of the behavior in question has been kept, as well as its frequency relative to other behaviors for that individual and a broader sample of individuals. Within the classroom, then, we may decide to observe a number of times during different periods of the day, as well as on different days of the week, and within the different behavioral settings available — classroom, gym, playground, and so on. Task 11 will test your ability to take a representative sample.

TASK 11: DETERMINING REPRESENTATIVE OBSERVATIONAL SAMPLES

Indicate which of the samples given on the Task 11 Worksheet are likely to yield representative observations. Check your responses with the sample responses given in the Appendix.

Who is sampled?   In addition to systematic sampling of behaviors, it is frequently necessary to sample pupils. For example, if our purpose were to determine whether or not kindergarten pupils in a particular school system encountered difficulty with letter recognition, we would not need to observe every child. Rather, we might want to select for study a random, unbiased sample of 10 pupils (for example, every third pupil according to last name in alphabetical order, or we could write the children's names on slips of paper, place them in a hat, and draw out our random sample of 10 pupils) from each of the kindergarten classrooms in the school system. On the other hand, for diagnostic purposes, an individual teacher may wish to observe every pupil's skills.

Another observer, interested in observing first-grade pupils' spontaneous use of relational terms such as "more" and "less" may, in a representative first-grade classroom, observe five pupils for 10 minutes, and so on until all pupils have been observed. This cycle may be repeated several times.

A useful sampling system reported by Kowatrakul (1959), which is referred to as point-time sampling, allows the observer to view a pupil long enough to record one of a given series of behaviors, then move on to the next pupil until a given behavior occurs, and so on. Kowatrakul has used this technique to study the relation between pupil behavior and classroom activities in various subject areas.

RECORDING OBSERVATIONAL DATA

An essential component of the observation process is the immediate recording of the behaviors observed. As noted in our discussion of time and event sampling, the observer cannot depend on memory; rather, the

TASK 11 WORKSHEET

Determining Representative Samples

Problem or Question	Behavior Sample	Representative?		Reasons for Your Response
		Yes	No	
Study of first-grade children's "on task" behavior in school.	Observe the behavior of children sitting in a front-row seat of each row in a particular class.			
Count of out-of-seat behaviors of an "acting-out" kindergartner.	Observe the child on five successive days from 10:00 a.m. to 10:15 a.m.			
Study the extent to which four-year-old children interact in same-sex, opposite-sex, or mixed-sex groupings on the playground.	Randomly choose four boys and four girls. Observe each child's behavior on a systematic rotation basis for five minutes, indicating the amount of time each child interacts in designated categories. Sampling should be done on different days and at different times.			

observer must use a recording sheet, if reliable data are to be collected. This recording sheet needs to be designed so that the information can be easily summarized. Although a broad variety of recording sheets can be found in the literature, the Flanders Interaction Analysis Categories (Simon & Boyer, 1969), a category system for collecting teacher–pupil interactions, involve the use of simple recording procedures.

The Flanders system has been one of the most widely used observation schemes and is commonly taught to teachers, student teachers, supervisors, and counselors who want to view and understand their typical patterns of verbal exchange with students in the classroom. Flanders offers 10 categories* for classifying verbal behaviors, which are shown in Figure 8.5. Flanders simply numbers the 10 categories sequentially from 1 to 10. By memorizing the code, the observer need only write down a single number to represent a type of verbal activity. The observer can write a stream of numbers that represent what is occurring in the classroom. As Simon and Boyer have noted, the observer "will have no record of what has been said but he will have a record which allows him to infer the classroom climate and describe the teaching style" (1969, p. 116). In recording observations, the observer makes a notation for every change in category and also records one category number at least every three seconds whether there is a category change or not.

Figure 8.5.   Flanders' Categories for Classifying Behavior

Category Number		Description
	1	Accepts pupils' feelings
	2	Praises or encourages pupils
Teacher	3	Accepts pupils' ideas
Talk	4	Asks questions
	5	Lectures
	6	Gives directions
	7	Criticizes or justifies authority
Student	8	Student talk—narrow response
Talk	9	Student talk—broad response
	10	Silence or noise (Simon & Boyer, 1969, pp. 118-19)

Source: A. Simon and E. G. Boyer, (Eds.). *Mirrors for behavior: An anthology of classroom observation instruments.* Philadelphia: Research for Better Schools, 1967, 1970.

---

*Flanders (1970) also discusses a "22 category system," which is a more extensive subdivision of the basic 10 categories.

A data sheet for one minute of consecutive observation and sequential coding of teacher–pupil verbal behaviors using the Flanders system would look like the sample record shown in Figure 8.6. By reading down the columns of numbers collected by the observer, one gets a picture of the sequence of verbal behaviors that occurred during the one-minute time period. After collecting these "raw" observational data over a more representative time sample than one minute, the observer can transcribe the data to a summary grid that provides a "picture" of the frequency of various kinds of teacher and pupil verbal activity occurring in the classroom setting.*

The observer can easily compute the percentage of time during the observation period that a particular kind of verbal behavior occurred. Also, by summarizing the observational data, the pattern or strategies used by a teacher in the classroom can be revealed. Questions such as the following can be answered with the Flanders system:

How often do pupils talk in the classroom?
How much do pupils talk in comparison with their teacher?
Do pupils talk to each other or only to the teacher?
How does the teacher reinforce different kinds of student verbal behavior?
What strategies does the teacher employ to involve students in classroom discussion? (Simon & Boyer, 1969, p. 120)

Figure 8.6.   Verbal Behaviors Data Sheet

Setting: Mrs. Jones Third-grade class	Date: June 3
Activity: Social Studies Discussion	Time: 10:50 to 10:51 a.m.

(1) 4	(5) 5	(9) 7	(13) 5	(17) 7
(2) 9	(6) 6	(10) 7	(14) 9	(18) 7
(3) 9	(7) 9	(11) 6	(15) 9	(19) 4
(4) 4	(8) 7	(12) 5	(16) 9	(20) 4

(Digits following numbers in parentheses indicate code.)

---

*It is generally recommended that a 20-minute observation (400 tallies) be used as a reasonable minimum for generating a picture of the verbal activity in a classroom. Simon and Boyer (1969) offer an excellent detailed description of the procedures for transcribing Flanders categories to a summary matrix.

By using the Flanders approach with these questions, the observer can begin to draw conclusions about classroom climate and make inferences about the communication strategies fostered in the classroom. Extensive information can be generated from a simple, sequential recording of category numbers on the page. The Flanders approach has been the forerunner of a wide range of observational techniques for the study of teaching and learning processes in educational settings (Evertson & Green, 1986). We have presented the Flanders system because of its simplicity and usefulness.

OTHER RECORDING FORMATS

In this section, two other sample recording formats are given. Both formats can be easily adapted by the teacher-observer to suit his or her own particular observation goal, as in the filled-out example on language use during free play (see Figure 8.8).

With Sample Worksheet A (Figure 8.7), the observer can:

Figure 8.7. Sample Worksheet A

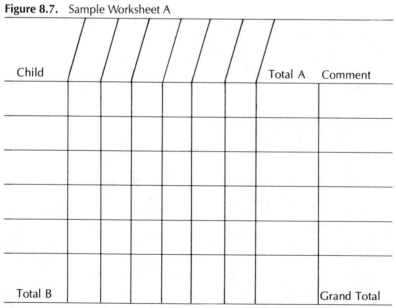

Total A is total of all observed behaviors demonstrated by a particular child.
Total B is total for each unit of behavior observed for all of the children combined.
Grand Total is total of all observed behaviors.

Figure 8.8. Language Usage During Free Play

Child	Uses Complete Sentences	Asks Questions for Information	Uses Relational Concepts			Total A	Comment
Jack Brown	IIII	‖‖ I	0				
Maryanne Jones	0	‖I	II				
Total B						Grand Total	

Detail the units or categories of behavior that constitute a particular area of concern (columns)

List those children to be observed (rows)

Tally the frequency of observed behaviors for each child (total across each row)

Tally the frequency of each behavior for all of the children observed (total across each column)

Total all observed behaviors (total rows × total columns)

In using this worksheet, the observer would list the categories of behavior to be observed in the diagonal columns across the top of the form.

The format given on Sample Worksheet A can be used with both category and sign systems, and is easily adaptable to recording observations over time. If one were to use different colored pencils in tallying behaviors at different times, one could quickly "eyeball" differences among children and by the same child at different times.

By using the format of Worksheet A, we have recorded some observations about the language used by two students during free play (see Figure 8.8). Verbally transcribing the observations, we learn that during the observation period Maryanne never used complete sentences but used relational terms; Jack used complete sentences, but did not use relational terms. We also learn that both Maryanne and Jack asked questions, but that Jack asked more questions.

Sample Worksheet B (Figure 8.9) provides a format an observer could use to note the variety of behaviors engaged in by one child or by a group of children throughout the course of a school day. The specific behaviors or particular activities that are to be observed would be listed in the diagonal columns at the center of the worksheet. This section could, of course, be extended to include as many activities or behaviors as the observer wanted to note. The "Observation Begins" and "Observation Ends" columns enable the observer to continue using one worksheet while major shifts in classroom activity occur.

As an example of how to use Sample Worksheet B, consider the steps a teacher would take when observing patterns of cooperative behavior in a classroom:

Define the variety of behaviors that indicate cooperation.
List these categories of behavior (or activities) in the diagonal columns across the top of the worksheet.

Figure 8.9.   Sample Worksheet B

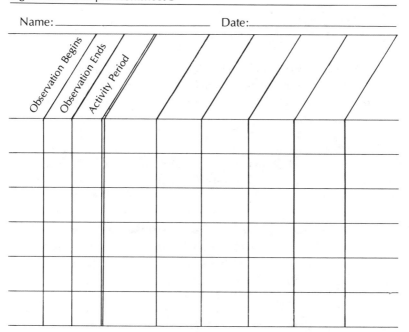

When beginning to observe, indicate the time.

Note the activity period in progress.

Tally the occurrence of each category of activity that occurs in the
appropriate column.

Note the time each observation period ends.

The observer would repeat the entire process using a sufficient number
of observation periods to adequately answer the question posed. In
using this worksheet, the observer would list the behaviors or activities
to be observed in the diagonal columns across the top of the form.

Worksheet A and Worksheet B provide a sample of the types of
simple instruments that can be devised for recording and organizing
observational information. Planning systematic recording procedures
ahead of time both facilitates observation and allows later review and
analysis. Remember, however, that although graphic representation can
be helpful in certain situations, the observer may also want to form
profiles or determine percentages and ratios that reflect the relative
frequency of particular kinds of behavior.

We have not attempted here to list all forms of recording systems
useful in educational settings. As you begin to grapple with a variety of
observation questions, you will create personal variations.

MAKING VALID OBSERVATIONS

Observational efforts will be in vain if what is observed and recorded does not correspond to real events. The validity of observations depends on how representative the record is of what actually occurred.
Systematic categories of behaviors and clear definitions of the behaviors
facilitate the objective classification of units of behavior and increase
the observer's consistency or reliability. We might, however, still have an
observation record that does not adequately reflect the real world, as
evidenced in cases of biased observations. We focus on this important
issue by regularly asking:

- What am I trying to sample from the stream of all behavior?
- Why am I interested in the particular information provided by
  the observation procedures I choose?
- Am I reporting what I see objectively?
- Have unintentional sources of bias been introduced?

Once again the particular problem or question raised and the observer's knowledge of that area will affect answers to these questions,

and particularly influence the format of the observations made. The validity of our observational measurements of behavior depends at least on these two conditions:

- A representative sample of the behaviors to be measured must be observed.
- A complete, accurate record of the observed behaviors must be made.

In recording and synthesizing observations, while taking into account those procedures that facilitate reliable and valid observations, the major problem that confronts the observer is the observer himself or herself. Drawing conclusions and solving problems demand that observers make inferences after digesting the information gathered during the observation process. Observers relate observations to the variables studied (for example, aggression, anxiety, motivation, and so forth), bringing behavior and construct together by inference. For example, an observer sees a child hitting another child and comes to the conclusion (inference) that the behavior is an example of hostility or aggression. The basic weakness of this process is that incorrect inferences can be made from observations. For example, two or more independent observers will note that in certain neighborhoods, white families move out as black families move in, and arrive at the inference that property values have gone down. The observation that white families are moving out and black families are moving in may be reliable and valid. However, an analysis of property values may show that in fact they have not decreased. Therefore, although certain behavior was observed, the conclusion that property values have gone down is invalid and subject to challenge. To judge property values, one should observe the price paid by all families who move in.

Another troublesome issue has to do with the number of observations required to support our inferences. How often and in what context must a child physically strike another child, for example, before we draw conclusions about the first child's "aggressive" nature or "hostile" manner? Although the answer to this particular question will vary extensively according to the point of view of the observer, the answer will be greatly influenced by the observer's intimate knowledge and understanding of the observed behaviors.

Making Interpretations

When we make inferences or draw conclusions from observational data, we are making *interpretations*, or adding meaning to the observations. Interpretations grow out of theories, past experiences, and present observations (McCutcheon, 1981). They "make sense" out of what we see and help us "understand" what we observed. There are at least three kinds of interpretations:

1. Forming *patterns* among observations, such as inferring the apparent order and rules for doing things in a classroom.
2. Interpreting the *social importance and meaning* of observed behaviors; for example, McCutcheon (1981) notes:

> We might observe students nodding during a [class presentation]. The physical behavior might be described as students moving their heads slightly, in an up and down motion. . . . What does this nodding mean? (p. 7)

The nods may signify different things. Are the pupils following the teacher's thoughts; agreeing with the teacher; feigning an interest that is not there, to be polite; falling asleep; or demonstrating a habit?
3. Relating observations to *external considerations* such as theories, philosophy, and historical events.

In interpreting observations, one might emphasize one type of interpretation over the others. The meaning that comes from interpreting observations grows out of the transaction between what we observed and what we have experienced. Thus, interpretation is in part subjective and in part objective.

The Types of Validity

As inferences and interpretations are arrived at and generalizations made on the basis of observational data, one should consider the various types of validity usually required of other assessment devices and techniques: concurrent validity, content validity, predictive validity, and construct validity.*

Concurrent validity. How do the observed behaviors relate to other external criteria such as test scores, school performance records, and parent reports? These concurrent data, independent of the observations, can help substantiate or validate the inference. For example, from

---

*See Cone (1982), Hoge (1985), and Kent & Foster (1977) for additional readings in this area.

observing that a child's distractibility is increased and her concentration decreased during unstructured group activities, we might conclude that the child does not respond productively to an unstructured situation. Independent psychological test data might suggest that the child has abilities to attend to detail and concentrate on such tasks as block design or puzzles (subtests on the Wechsler Intelligence Scale for Children — Revised) when these are presented in a one-to-one situation. This finding would provide substantiating evidence that the child is capable of being attentive when confronted with the appropriate context or situation. The more independent evidence accumulated to support inferences based on observation, the more credible and valid the inferences become.

Content validity.   Does the observation adequately sample or represent the behavior of concern? Has the observation question been refined sufficiently? Are the categories of observation exhaustive of the problem at hand? Content validity is the most fundamental form of validity for observational procedures.

Predictive validity.   How do observational outcomes relate to or predict future performance? Sources of information at a future time might include test scores, grades, or classroom performance.

Construct validity.   Perhaps the most important question the developer of an observational instrument must ask is: Do the target behaviors observed in fact tap or represent the psychological constructs — for example, "independence," "creativity," "role-taking ability," "intelligence," and so forth — that are of particular interest to the observer?

DETERMINING THE APPROPRIATENESS OF AN OBSERVATION SYSTEM

Figure 8.10 gives a list of questions an observer should ask about the observation about to be made, the technique to be employed, and its appropriateness. After some experience, these questions should occur to the observer as a matter of course and it will no longer be necessary to consult the checklist.

It is most essential for observers to evaluate their observation needs before adopting the use of a published research instrument or observation technique. The array of observation schedules available to the class-

Figure 8.10. Checkpoints for Determining the Appropriateness of an Observation System

---

1 For what purpose was the system developed?
   A. Does the stated purpose match your goal?
   B. What will be observed (behavioral definition)?
   C. Is the procedure limited by a particular theoretical perspective?

2 Are the conditions for observer reliability met?
   A. Behaviors to be viewed are sufficiently specified so as to be:
   Mutually exclusive (do not overlap each other). Exhaustive* (all behaviors of concern can be classified, but the need for exhaustive categories depends on the purpose of a particular observation).
   B. Categories are sufficiently narrow so that two or more observers will place an observed behavior into the same category.
   C. Is observer interpretation necessary or not?
   D. What reliability data are presented?

3 What type of system is employed?
   A. Category system: Every unit of behavior observed is categorized into one of the categories specified.
   B. Sign system: Selected behavioral units, listed beforehand, may or may not actually be observed during a period of time.

4 Are appropriate sampling procedures employed?
   A. The procedure for sampling behaviors is systematic:
   Time sampling—occurrence or nonoccurrence of behaviors within specified uniform time units.
   Event sampling—event recorded each time it occurs.
   B. Is the procedure feasible?
   How do you sample individuals to be observed?
   In what period of time?
   Is the desired detail possible given the number of individuals and time units?
   C. What is the coding system like?
   How complex is the system?
   Do tallies or codes require memorization? If coding required, is code indicated on the record form?
   What is the recording format like?
   D. Are the behaviors to be viewed representative?
   How many behaviors are to be viewed?
   Over what period of time?
   Using how many subjects?

5 Are the conditions for validity met?
   Are the behaviors you observe relevant to the inferences and interpretations you make?
   Have sources of observer bias been eliminated?

6 What training procedures are necessary to learn the system?

7 If studies have been reported using the system, what are their outcomes?

8 What modifications will you need to make to the system to adapt it to your purpose?

---

room observer often confuses the consumer as to the appropriateness of one structured approach versus another for a given educational situation. Among the most useful resources for helping evaluate a given observational procedure are the *Mirrors for Behavior* anthologies prepared by Simon and Boyer (1967, 1970, 1974), Evertson and Green's chapter in the *Third Handbook of Research on Teaching* (1986), and Foster and Cone's chapter in the *Handbook of Behavioral Assessment* (1986). Gordon and Jester (1973) have reviewed techniques of observing teaching in early childhood settings, which include home and day-care settings as well as preschool classrooms. Finally, Boyer, Simon, and Karafin (1973) have edited an anthology of early childhood observation instruments.

ETHICAL ISSUES IN OBSERVATION

Given the current climate in which the public has seriously questioned such school activities as psychological testing and other forms of assessment and record-keeping without prior parental permission or knowledge, we must consider the point at which observation techniques may interfere with an individual's privacy and rights. We cannot deny that individuals routinely and legitimately observe each of us in our daily activities. Depending on the nature of the stated purpose of the observation, if someone is observed without being made aware of this or without prior permission such observations may well constitute an invasion of privacy. In the case of the young child, receiving parental permission is an appropriate consideration. However, as children become more aware of their rights, even though it may affect the results of our data collection, it is necessary to seriously consider informing the child of our intent to observe (Russell Sage Foundation, 1969).

Most classroom observers do not invade a child's privacy. A teacher observes children as they work in a variety of classroom learning situations in order to develop more effective teaching strategies, and violation occurs only if the data collection goes beyond this function. A student teacher observes in classrooms to gain an understanding of appropriate teaching behaviors and of child development. The special educator observes the effectiveness of an intervention. The school psychologist observes a child with a behavior problem to better understand the nature of the problem and the classroom conditions that might be contributing factors.

Social scientists, child development researchers, and educators have struggled with the question of privacy and the possible uses to which data can be put, however well-intentioned the observation process may have been originally. The American Psychological Association, in its *Ethical Principles in the Conduct of Research with Human Participants* (1981), places much covert observation and recording into the category of invasion of privacy. Tape recordings, videotapings, and other mechanical recordings — although facilitating the collection of more comprehensive observation information — must be used with such ethical considerations taken into account (see Unit X). The Society for Research in Child Development, in its *Ethical Standards for Research with Children* (1982), stresses the rights of the child and the need to respect a child's willingness or refusal to participate in research.

Like most ethical issues, the problem of invasion of privacy through observation techniques is a complex, multifaceted dilemma that cannot be resolved by simple answers (see Brandt, 1972). However, as we consider the value of observation skills as a method of inquiry and as a source for building inferences, we must constantly raise the question of ethics. (A number of important ethical concerns and procedures for conducting research with children in natural settings, such as informed consent and confidentiality, have been summarized by Rheingold, 1982).

The Teacher as Observer

Mrs. Paredes, a teacher in a first-grade classroom, is concerned about the behavior of Gregory. He frequently becomes restless and cries in class. In attempting to understand this behavior, Mrs. Paredes decides to observe at what time of the school day, during what activities, and with what frequency Gregory becomes restless and cries.

The school social worker periodically visits the classroom of Mr. Green, making anecdotal records of student behaviors possibly indicating drug usage.

Mrs. Morris, a housemother for young children at a residential treatment center, is concerned with the health and physical care of the eight children for whom she is responsible. Each day of the week she systematically notes different physical features of the children such as their skin tone, hair, and fingernails to check that all is in order.

These examples provide us with some notion of the various ways in which observations are used in schools and school-related settings. Now that we have dealt with the major factors involving observation skills and in devising observation schedules, let us consider some additional issues in using systematic observation techniques in the classroom and developing observation schedules tailored to specific classroom problems.

THE TEACHER OR THE OUTSIDER AS OBSERVER

Although innovations such as team teaching and the use of classroom paraprofessionals have generated possibilities for individuals involved in the classroom to observe ongoing behavior, for the most part systematic observation has been carried out by the social worker, school psychologist, researcher, and other school personnel who are not integral members of the classroom setting. Generally, when teachers have used observation techniques, they have been unstructured and highly dependent on remembering the observed behaviors until an opportune time to record — usually the end of the day. However, there are a number of alternative approaches that can enable the teacher to implement structured and systematic observation procedures in the classroom.

- In collaboration with a team teacher, paraprofessional, or another classroom teacher with a free period, the teacher can develop an appropriate schedule for observing and in turn share observing responsibilities.
- When other personnel are not available, the teacher, again using an appropriate schedule, can decide to depart from the teaching routine and systematically observe during a certain portion of each day. For example, the teacher may determine to observe and record the variety of independent activities engaged in by class members. The observation might take place for five minutes at the beginning and five minutes at the end of the activities period each day over the course of a week. Children will be engaged in activities while the observation takes place. The amount of time required for observational activity is small in proportion to the benefits that can result from collecting the observation data. For example, to obtain information about the patterns of peer interaction within a classroom, the teacher might decide to observe a sample of five pupils as they interact with classmates; each pupil is observed for one minute during each of four hours (perhaps 9:00 and 11:00 A.M. and 1:00 and 3:00 P.M.) of the class day over a given number of days.
- The teacher can also function as a "participant-observer," recording observations while interacting with observed pupils. This type of observation, important in open classroom settings, involves the teacher in observing and recording teacher–pupil behaviors in a few predetermined categories over brief periods of time.

Problems Encountered by the Teacher as Observer

Even when the teacher is removed from the stream of behavior and fulfills the role of an observer in the classroom, his or her mere presence in the setting is bound to influence certain pupil behaviors to some extent. One probably would get different results if some other person, such as the principal, were in the classroom.

A more difficult problem, referred to as the "halo effect" (see also

Unit VII), involves the influence of the teacher's previous knowledge and experience with a classroom of pupils and their past behavior on making objective observations of current behavior. For example, from past experience, a teacher, anticipating that Donald is attentive and concentrates well in the classroom, will tend to ignore or underemphasize any instance of "off-task" behavior that Donald exhibits. As another example, many teachers, anticipating that children from lower socioeconomic groups have poor verbal expressive abilities, might overlook instances of excellent verbal expression in the classroom.

One way of tempering the influence of the halo effect is to involve additional independent observers at some point in the observation process to determine how valid the teacher's observations are. The assumption here is that an outside observer has not had previous experience with and expectations of the children involved.

SOLVING CLASSROOM PROBLEMS THROUGH OBSERVATION TECHNIQUES

We have presented a variety of examples from the classroom in which observation procedures might be used. Let us now consider some general problems that might be approached through observational techniques.

Determining the Effectiveness of Educational Programs and Curricula

Current teacher training programs, education literature, local school district programs, and the media have exposed teachers to a variety of innovations, theoretical orientations, and ways to deal with day-to-day learning and classroom behavior problems. Observation techniques can facilitate a teacher's adaptation and use of many of these "new" educational ideas. Before introducing a new program intended to produce changes in learning or other classroom behavior, the teacher should collect a baseline of observation data on behaviors that the program is aimed at influencing.

In the example presented in Figure 9.1 we are assuming that a classroom teacher intends to introduce a token reinforcement system aimed at increasing the amount of time the pupils in the class pursue assigned tasks. Before introducing the system it is essential that the teacher collect observation data on the relevant behavior. The baseline data are collected for days 1 and 2. The token system is introduced on

Figure 9.1. Charts for Numbers of Minutes Pupils Worked on Assigned Tasks

Pupil A

Day	Reading	Arithmetic	Spelling	Other Assignments	Total Time Pupil "On Task"	Total Time for Pupil Work on Assigned Tasks
1	20	20	5	10	55	110
2	18	20	4	8	50	120
3	22	18	12	13	65	100
4	25	22	18	19	84	120

*

Pupil B

Day	Reading	Arithmetic	Spelling	Other Assignments	Total Time Pupil "On Task"	Total Time for Pupil Work on Assigned Tasks
1	15	15	10	10	50	110
2	12	17	8	11	48	120
3	18	20	10	7	55	100
4	20	25	15	12	72	120

*

*Heavy rule indicates baseline.

day 3 and continues for a given period of time. The observations should continue to be made during this period to ascertain whether the pupils' on-task behavior has actually changed as a result of the program. Charts such as those shown in Figure 9.1 could be used for recording these observations over a number of days. (We are here showing the results for only four days and for only two pupils; an actual reinforcement system and the observations would naturally involve more pupils and a longer observation period.) On-task behavior is defined for this sample as the amount of time pupils work at assigned tasks.

After a sufficient number of days of observation, the teacher could calculate the percentage of on-task behavior for each pupil. This would be the total time the pupil worked divided by the length of working time available. The information recorded on the observation schedule could be transformed into a graph like that shown in Figure 9.2. Here, the total amount of time students could work at all assigned tasks on day 3 was 100 minutes. Pupil A was observed to be on task for a total of 65 minutes. By dividing these 65 minutes by the 100 minutes of total working time we see that pupil A was on task 65 percent of the time on day 3. By the same method of computation, we found the percentage of on-task behavior for day 4, and plotted these figures on the graph. The same procedure was followed for pupil B.

In Figure 9.2, days 1 and 2 yield the baseline information on the percentage of on-task behavior demonstrated by both pupils prior to the introduction of the reinforcement system. If the token program works, the percentage of on-task behavior should increase as the percentages on the graph seem to indicate: from this graph, the teacher could conclude that the on-task behavior of pupils A and B has increased as a result of the token program. To verify this conclusion the teacher should eliminate the reinforcement system and observe whether or not there is a decrease in on-task behavior. After confirmation of the reinforcement system's impact on behavior, the teacher would reintroduce the token program, expecting another increase in on-task behavior of the students.

STUDYING DEVELOPMENTAL DIFFERENCES IN CHILDREN

Observation techniques can provide an effective means of conveying to teachers the basic differences that exist among children at various developmental levels. Often teachers — particularly those just out of teacher training programs — have difficulty setting appropriate expectations and goals for children of different ages in their classes. Making systematic observations of children at successive age levels can provide

Figure 9.2. Graph for Percent of "On Task" Behavior

Percent	Day 1	Day 2	Day 3	Day 4	Additional Days of Program
100					
95					
90					
85					
80					
75					
70					
65					
60					
55					
50					
45					
40					

Key: Pupil A:——   Pupil B: . . . . .

an effective approach to understanding the behavioral differences demonstrated by children at different ages. For example, although the three-year-old can be observed having difficulty tying his shoelaces, the seven-year-old child not only performs this task with ease, but also demonstrates facility in many other fine motor activities. The typical five-year-old, viewing an airplane in the sky, is unable to describe its real size or rate of speed; however, by 10 years of age, the child is capable of understanding the effects of distance on size and speed. With an appreciation of the basic differences in cognitive, emotional, and motor behaviors of children at different ages, the teacher has a sounder basis on which to base instruction and build curricula.

Diagnostic Assessment of Learning Activity

Certain classroom assessment procedures are variations of systematic event samplings, where the events or problems are presented to each pupil and the teacher observes each pupil's strategy in dealing with them. The teacher may observe each child at the blackboard working on a multiplication problem involving two-place carrying of numbers, noting that one child has difficulty applying the carrying strategy per se, while another child has difficulty lining up numbers. In order to do such an assessment systematically, the teacher should prepare beforehand a list of relevant learning strategies and errors that can occur on this task and then focus on them in making the observations, as shown in Figure 9.3.

Observing each child perform a task such as the multiplication problem allows the teacher to view the child's approach to a learning situation, in contrast to the more typical situation in which the child, working alone on his or her worksheet, might make some errors. In the latter situation, it is difficult to identify why the child had trouble

Figure 9.3. Multiplication of Two-Place Problems with Carrying

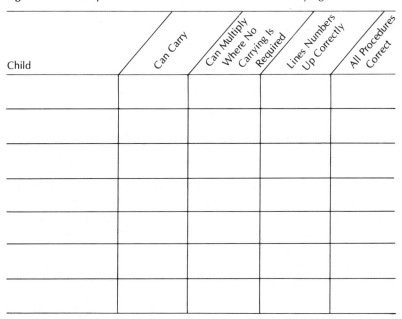

Child	Can Carry	Can Multiply Where No Carrying Is Required	Lines Numbers Up Correctly	All Procedures Correct

solving the problem. Only through observing the problem-solving process can the teacher know precisely what kind of help a given child might need.

STEPS TO MAKING CLASSROOM OBSERVATIONS

Following is an overview of the various steps the classroom teacher should take in developing a useful observation system. In following these steps, the observer can be aware of the nature of observations and have greater confidence in the inferences and decisions generated as a result of observation activity. An application example follows the description of each step.

1. What is the nature of the problem or the question with which you are confronted? Define the problem and the related behaviors clearly.

> The first-grade teachers at a school located within a large metropolitan area have established a resource center for their pupils. The purpose of the center is to provide an opportunity for the first-graders to engage in a variety of learning activities, focusing on the development of beginning reading skills. Each of the school's three first-grade classes spends approximately 25 minutes of each day in the center. During this time, the children complete one task that they have individually selected from a series of 30 learning activities: copying shapes, matching letters with objects depicting that letter name, classifying objects into concept categories, listening to an audiotape of a story while looking at pictures of that story, and so on. When a child completes a learning activity and has the project checked by the teacher or aide, the child may choose another task. The teachers want to know if their first-grade pupils are able to select, pursue, and complete these tasks independently of teacher, aide, or other pupil assistance.
>
> *Problem:* Do individual first-graders select, pursue, and complete the learning activities without seeking assistance of the teacher, aide, or other pupils?

2. Why should systematic observation be helpful in dealing with this problem or answering the question?

The teachers decide that by using observational procedures they will be able to make systematic recordings of the pupils' behavior during their time in the resource center. The teachers could limit their approach to merely looking at completed pupil activities, but by introducing observation of the patterns of pupil behavior in the center the teachers gather a richer pool of information for drawing their conclusions and more directly answering their question about pupil independence. Furthermore, observations over time will provide teachers with an understanding of differences among children in pursuing and completing activities without the assistance of others.

3. What are the relevant characteristics of the setting in which behavior will be observed? (Characteristics of the setting include space, equipment, and people present.)

- What constraints does the physical setting have on possible behaviors?

     Because the average first-grade class at the school consists of 25 children, and since a "standard"-sized classroom has been designated as the resource center, the pupils' behavior is limited in its range of mobility. Yet, because of pupil proximity, the setting itself might encourage verbal exchanges and pupils' "assisting" one another. Of course the availability of the particular learning materials, as opposed to other possible materials, can restrain the scope of behaviors to be viewed.

- What is the physical arrangement of the various components of the setting that might be considered?

     Each of 30 tasks are numbered and placed in various locations such as bookshelves, windowsills, corners of the floor, and on tables. Pupil work areas are provided adjacent to the materials.

- What people will be present in the setting? What characteristics of the individuals or group being observed need to be considered?

In addition to the 25 pupils in the first-grade class, a class teacher, an aide, and an observer are present in the setting. The aide has been trained beforehand in the use of the learning materials, but has been encouraged to provide assistance only when requested by pupils. The observer will be one of the other first-grade teachers who has arranged a 25-minute free period to coincide with the resource center period of this class.

4. Given the particular focus of your observations and given your knowledge of the problem area, what is the universe of behaviors that you intend to consider?

The teachers will consider how the pupils:
—Select an activity. (What task does a pupil choose on any given day? What is the range of tasks that he or she chooses over a period of time?)
—Engage in a task. (Do the pupils work with or without requesting assistance from teacher, teacher aide, or other pupils?)
—Indicate that a given task is completed.
     In addition, it might also be interesting to see if there is a relationship between these observed behaviors and the quality of the pupil's final product.

5. What units of behavior or clearly defined categories of behavior will you focus on?
   Analyze the behavior into its component parts. In determining your list of categories for classifying observable behavior, consider whether a previously developed observational schedule might be used. Decide whether a sign or category system is more appropriate for your problem:
   — Are the categories or signs employed mutually exclusive?
   — Is the listing of categories or signs exhaustive of the universe of behaviors you wish to consider?

In their search of observational schedules already available for use, the teachers were unable to find a recording system including the categories of behaviors that matched the purpose of their observations.
     Since they were interested in evidence of independent behavior, they adopted a sign system; that is, they generated

the following specific categories of behavior for labeling observations:

—The child selects one of the 30 activities, then picks up the materials and takes them to the designated work area. (However, if the child merely looks at the materials without taking them to the work area, this would not be classified as selecting a task.)

—The child requests assistance from the teacher, aide, or another pupil in the resource center by either gesturing for assistance, verbally asking for assistance, or combining gesture and verbal request. (However, if the child asks to get a drink of water or merely talks to the teacher, aide, or another pupil, this would not be classified as a request for assistance.)

—The child indicates that a given task has been completed by showing the product to the teacher or aide. (However, if the child partially completes the task, he or she would be encouraged to resume work on the task—but this would not constitute a request for assistance.)

6. What sampling procedure (time or event) will most effectively enable you to record representative observations?

   • Will all the people in the setting be observed, or will you select a representative sample?

      The teachers decided which children would be observed and at what frequency. Since it would be impossible for an individual teacher to observe all children simultaneously, it is necessary to observe a sample of children each day and to order the observations of their behavior systematically. Therefore, the teachers adopted a time-sampling procedure—that is, they decided to observe a preselected sample of five children each day. Consequently, by the end of a five-day school week each of the 25 children will have been observed during one of the daily sessions in the resource center.

   • How frequently across time should you observe so that your conclusions have adequate observational support?

      In order to observe each of the five children at different points in the work period, the teacher-observer observes each of the five children to be observed that day at work for one minute during a five-minute segment. The teacher then proceeds to observe each of the five for one minute for the second five-minute segment, and so forth until each of the five children has been observed for a total of four minutes. This procedure is followed each day of the week, five children at a time, until all 25 children have been observed.

- To what extent does the subject of the observation need to be viewed in a variety of settings and activities within the school in order to deal adequately with the particular problem or question? (Does not apply to this particular observation problem.)

7. Design a recording format. (See Figure 9.4 for sample.)
8. How confident are you that your observation schedule facilitates reliable observations? How might you verify this?

To determine the reliability of the observational scheme, two of the three first-grade teachers might observe the resource center period of the third teacher on two consecutive days. The degree to which the two raters agreed with each other in recording the instances of request for assistance could then be determined. The percentage of agreement in indicating the pupil's selection of tasks could also be determined by this procedure. A high rate of agreement would indicate a high level of reliability between the observers.

9. What inferences or conclusions can you make on the basis of your collected observation data?

Conclusions can be arrived at regarding:
—What tasks were chosen? By how many pupils?
—Which tasks were completed? By how many pupils?
—Were certain chosen tasks completed more often than others?
—How often did pupils request assistance? Which children requested assistance? From whom?
—Were there differences among the three classes observed?
—What inferences can be made about the use of the resource center?

Figure 9.4. Sample Recording Sheet for Observations in Resource Center

Week 1, Day 1　　　　　Date:　　　　　20-minute period

| Child | Activity Selected | Frequency of Requests for Assistance From:* | | | Requests for Check of Completed Activity |
		Teacher	Aide	Other Child	Total	
Total						

* Use sign system and wait for instances of behavior to occur

—Can the data be summarized in a graph or chart? The use of a graph or chart helps communicate to others the outcomes of observation.

10. Have you realized the goal for which your observations have been made? If not, can you redefine your problem more clearly and focus on different behaviors, and from a different perspective? (In other words, can you pilot an alternative approach?)

The example as developed should allow the teachers to answer the question posed in Point 1, although alternative approaches to the problem could be developed.

11. Did you consider the role that methods of inquiry other than systematic observation — psychometric testing, controlled experimentation, or developmental histories — might play in dealing with your problem? (Does not pertain to the example presented.)

The Relationship Between Media and Observation

In this unit we will consider briefly the interactions that take place between the observer and the medium of observation. Observation may take place in a live situation or through media — pictures, slides, film, videotape, printed materials, audio recordings, or any combination of these. Each medium has formal characteristics that affect the observation process, and each allows for certain predictions. For example, even the most skilled stenographer is unable to record all the innuendos of a single speaker with paper and pencil, and the task becomes more difficult with an increase in the number of simultaneous speakers. On the other hand, a tape recorder and appropriately placed microphones provide a record of all verbal interactions, even whispers. But the tape system would not pick up gestures or facial expressions. Each medium has its strengths and its limitations, a topic to be covered in greater detail later in this unit.

THE "MECHANICS" OF MEDIA AND THE OBSERVER

Several interacting factors need to be taken into account when considering the use of media. They include:

- Availability of media equipment
- Ease of use (operation)
- Degree of special training required
- Ease of recording (encoding) and gaining appropriate information from that recording (decoding)
- Range of applicability
- Cost
- Intrusiveness of the media system

This unit was written with the help of John L. Swayze.

For example, paper and pencil are almost always available and require no training, but are limited in their applicability without other aids. On the other hand, mechanical sound recording provides a much more complete account of a given situation, but requires costly equipment, which is often inaccessible, necessitates some training to operate, and can intrude on the setting. The question of intrusiveness is important in the choice of media for observational purposes. A behavioral measure of intrusiveness might well be the amount of time required for the subjects of the observation to ignore the presence of the observation system itself.

The still picture or single photograph, while generally easy to obtain, is one of the most difficult observation representations to interpret, due to the minimal sample of behaviors, situations, or actions obtained. The viewer frequently does not know what occurred immediately before or immediately after the incident photographed. The motion picture, by contrast, falls toward the other extreme of the picture-sampling dimension. It normally exposes from 18 to 24 still pictures per second, providing a more complete representation for interpretation. The more complete representation results from the dense sample of situations, behaviors, or actions presented in rapid sequence during a brief span of time. The motion picture, by presenting many frames per second to the observer, reduces the number of inferences required by the observer.

Actually, more information is available in motion pictures than most viewers use. For example, a frame by frame analysis would allow the viewer to look at eye movement. Slow motion presentation and repeated showings would allow other analyses. The viewer in most film-watching situations does not have time to extract all the information available. In fact, the viewer's perception is usually controlled by the filmmaker or by the purpose for which the film is viewed.

Differences, such as those between the still picture and motion picture, exist among all media and should be considered when choosing among them. The obvious differences of sound, motion, and nonmotion occur immediately to most people. The subtle differences, however, also influence the nature of data.

The ideal observation tool does not yet exist. Such a tool would provide a "magical time machine" display that would allow the observer to be invisible, to control the speed and direction of time, move backward and forward in time, freeze time, and review at will, and have all senses represented. With such a device the observer might well have the sensation of being on the scene without being part of it.

ADVANTAGES AND DISADVANTAGES
OF THE MEDIA OF OBSERVATION

First-Hand Observation

Direct viewing of a given situation provides more information than any individual can deal with at a given time. Therefore, a conscious selection process determines the foci of one's observations. Other information is screened out and what is viewed is ordered to conform with the frames of reference brought to that situation. Thus, an observer concerned about the physical manifestations of nutrition in a group of young children would focus on physical and behavioral features such as skin tone, fingernails, hair, weight, alertness, and energy level, while screening out verbal interchanges between children and the type of objects chosen for play.

The advantages of first-hand observation include:

- The immediacy of the information gained.
- The wide range of information available.
- The flow of action present — the viewer can see, hear, or inquire about what happened immediately prior to or following any given instance.

The advantages of direct observation are also the sources of its limitations:

- The screening out of some behaviors while focusing on others.
- The human factor — individual biases or prejudices, memory of events, inappropriate foci.
- The effect of the observer's presence on the events being observed.

The presence of more than one trained observer in a given situation can solve some of the problems posed above but introduces others, including cost in time and potential interference with the ongoing process. Thus, the human being without the help of other techniques is restricted in his or her capacity to collect data in a live situation. The introduction of categorized recording systems, rating scales, pictorial records, and sound recordings can help an individual's perceptions become more than somewhat unreliable impressions. With certain strengths and weaknesses, some of them unique to the medium under consideration, the use of the media of observation is introduced. Although no single medium can combine all of the strengths of human observation, various media can be combined and compensate for some of the weaknesses.

The Still Picture or Slide

A picture or series of pictures, although reflecting the selectivity of the photographer, does permit the viewer to reexamine the picture in order to test his or her own perception and interpretation of that picture. The viewer can examine the order or sequence of behaviors or actions shown to infer, for example, that motion or change took place. The picture or series of pictures also allows the viewer to compare his or her own observations with those made by others of the same events, and to review the depicted events at some future time. The observation process can thus be extended beyond the limitations of the observing human being. The ability to review the stimuli provides the primary advantage of the single still picture or sequence of pictures over direct observation.

The major limitation of a single picture or slide is the obvious one: It presents a static view of the instance, forcing the viewer to seek additional information or to make inferences without knowing what immediately preceded or followed the event. A second limitation is that in most cases the photographer makes the selection for the viewer. A useful comparison might well be made between the still picture and a painting: An individual looking at a painting tends to seek subtle meaning in it, whereas the same individual viewing a photograph often accepts it as total reality, when it is in fact a partial representation of reality. One way to deal with this problem is to use a sequence of still pictures. Each additional picture, in sequence, clarifies the scene, setting, interactions, and outcomes.

The teacher, then, may find a "before" and "after" photo useful, or may wish to photograph a sequence of events. Photographic surveys of classrooms can provide teachers with detailed understanding of classroom environments. Adis (1977), for example, used a photographic survey to identify patterns of student interaction with classroom resources. Photographs of classrooms were taken and coded through use of a locational grid and computerized blueprint of each classroom. Thus it was possible to track patterns of student interaction with classroom resources and with other students. More simple recordings can involve photographing each activity area of the room and the classroom clock on a regular basis during a day—for example, every 15 minutes during an entire day.

Audio Recordings

With appropriately placed microphones and adequate equipment, audiotape recordings can provide a flexible record of verbal interchanges in a situation. To evaluate a conversation one might focus on content analysis, phonemic analysis, volume-level shift, pacing, and expression. In the live situation the hearer-observer would never be able to absorb and analyze the conversation from these varied foci. The recording, because of its *playback* characteristic, allows for other analyses, and in this way provides a major contribution to the repertoire of observation tools.

When sound recordings are transcribed, considerable information is lost, for the innuendos of expression, pace, and intonation are difficult to retain once the conversation is in typescript. Audio recordings alone also have limitations in comparison with those of pictorial recordings. There is a loss of the information obtained from facial expressions or other body movements (which might be in contrast to what is spoken), the behavior of others, and the setting. On the positive side of the coin, however, the transcriptions can be reviewed and recorded in an objective manner. In combination with other media, sound recording contributes usefully to the completeness of the recorded representation.

Films and Videotapes

A 16mm sound film or a videotape provides the most complete recording of most situations, since auditory, visual, and time dimensions are accounted for, but the observer tends to be more passive while viewing film and is subject to the selectivity of the filmmaker. Furthermore, there is ample room for viewer selectivity to come into play, for viewers will bring their own biases, training, and experiences to viewing the film. Sound film has the specific advantages of high density and flexibility: Film and videotape can be viewed frame by frame, stopped at a given frame, replayed, and reviewed by many observers. Therefore, this is a very useful form both for purposes of training and for analyzing data. Use of computer analysis facilitates highly detailed accounts of behavior. Future use of interactive videodiscs will further enhance the use of observational sequences.

The major limitations to the use of sound film and videotape derive from the cost and the technical competency required for quality production. Recent advances in technology have eliminated some of these problems. Schools increasingly have videotape equipment that can be borrowed for classroom use. Observers using videotapes need to keep in mind, however, that important behaviors can still be missed, depending on the angle of the camera and the activity level of the child. Young children move frequently and do not necessarily face the camera. Equipment can break down, the noise level of a room might be high, or one can forget to turn the camera on.

Despite these cautions, film and videotape can greatly enhance our understanding of young children, including the processes and strategies they use to solve problems. Kounin (1975), for example, videotaped child behaviors both in free play and in formal lesson settings. Teachers' communication style, use of materials and visual aids, and pupil behaviors such as listening and responding to a story all influenced the success of lessons. Ginsburg (1987) has used videotape to investigate young children's understanding of number. He is developing teacher workshop packages built around these videotapes that focus on strategies children use to solve number problems, the kinds of errors they make, and how they explain these errors. Following a child's response, an interviewer poses questions such as "How did you figure out your answer?" or "How did you know?" Although the child might respond "Because I am smart," important clues might be revealed from the tape regarding the child's skills. Teachers and parents can develop considerable insight through observing and discussing such videotaped sequences.

For us as adults, the Iranian hostage crisis in 1980 provided a poignant example of how film and videotape might be used to deal with a politically volatile, life-and-death situation: Governmental officials studied film clips of the hostages for clues to the hostages' mental states. Among the questions the observers presumably asked were:

> What did the background voices say while the hostages were speaking?
> Were all the relatives mentioned real?
> Were there hidden messages in the hostages' statements?
> Was there evidence of drug influence in the ways the hostages moved their arms, legs, and eyes?
> What could be inferred about the extent of tension and anxiety through voice analysis?
> Which hostages had gained or lost weight?
> Were the hostages who helped themselves to the fruit so clearly displayed on camera those who might have been imprisoned or kept in solitary confinement?

Other nonverbal activities might have provided meaningful information as well.

Black and White or Color

We live in a chromatic world and when we view situations first hand, the chromatic qualities are of course retained. The degree to which visual media can reproduce the chromatic qualities of first-hand observations varies. Color reproductions have a different information-carrying capacity than black and white reproductions. For example, look again at the photograph of the supermarket scene for Task 2 near the start of Unit IV and consider the additional information a color reproduction might have provided about the cleanliness of the store.

Color carries information but it can also dominate the viewer's perceptions and, depending on one's purposes, may need to be screened out. Since color adds greatly to the cost of reproduction, the advantages and disadvantages of its use must be a consideration.

The selection of appropriate data collection tools or media requires knowledge of their technology. Therefore, effective use of media in observation requires an understanding of the advantages and limitations of each medium with the end of maintaining as much control as possible. Accordingly, a useful ground rule is to have as much control as possible over the media used; at every point control is yielded, a degree of freedom is also yielded. Thus the viewer needs a knowledge of the repertoire of observation tools and media available and their unique characteristics. With such knowledge, one can choose the tool or tools most appropriate for a given purpose.

Mechanical Recording Systems

Counting devices, not unlike portable calculators, are available for recording the frequency of behaviors of interest. Microcomputer systems also allow the collection of data about individuals as they respond to program materials — concerning reaction time, errors made, branching, and the number of attempts to meet a criterion level (see Unit XI).

In summary, the observer needs to consider carefully the characteristics, advantages, and drawbacks of different media forms. Kent and Foster (1977) make the point that different media forms may not be equivalent or even comparable since they produce different kinds of data. However, the use of both audiotape and videotape or film greatly enhances our ability to review carefully the observation situation. Unless these media are an integral component of the environment, however, their introduction may be intrusive. A period of time to adjust to the presence of these nonhuman observers may be necessary.

The effects of different media on the resulting observational data have been summarized by Foster and Cone (1986), who point out that:

- Inter-observer agreement differs between live observation and when observing videotaped presentations. Depending on the target behaviors observed, agreement tends to be higher in live situations.
- Findings are not uniform across media.

Developing Observation Methods Appropriate to the Computer-Assisted Learning Environment

Observation in the electronic learning environment brings with it many of the same issues as observing in any learning environment, plus some additional challenges. The challenges arise from the fact that in the electronic learning environment the content and the process of learning become observable in new ways. On the microcomputer screen, we can see the content of what the student is working on: correct responses, errors, the amount of branching to more fundamental examples or to more difficult problems, and so forth. Another challenge arises from the fact that considerable activity occurs simultaneously, particularly in the three-way interaction that takes place between the teacher or tutor, the learner, and the computer software.

A rich literature in classroom observation has provided us with increased understanding of both teacher and learner behaviors (Evertson & Green, 1986). In these studies, observers have viewed behaviors from a number of perspectives:

- Focusing on learners in their natural environment in order to understand the development of the learner's behavioral repertoire, the process of classroom interaction, the problems learners encounter, and the approaches students take
- Studying the frequency or rate with which behaviors targeted for observation occur
- Understanding the circumstances that led up to target behaviors as well as what followed the behaviors

COMPUTER-ASSISTED TUTORING: USE OF COMPUTER SOFTWARE

In our book, attention has been centered on the *teacher* and *learner* and the interaction between the two. However, in the electronic learning environment, the computer software becomes a third focus of interest, and interactions among student, teacher, and computer become possible (Figure 11.1).

Understanding this three-way interaction can be a viable observational goal as we have learned from our own experiences in the Computer-Assisted Tutoring Service (CATS) at Teachers College, where children and tutors have worked together with commercially available software. For example, we were interested in understanding the exchanges among children, their tutors, and computer software; the motivational impact of the software; and the impact of the computer experience on the learning process. Questions that could be addressed through systematic observations were raised:

- Were learners on task?
- Was their attention maintained when they encountered difficulty?
- What did tutors do to enhance the learning situation?
- With what kinds of learning tasks were children successful, and where did they encounter difficulties?
- What characteristics of the software seemed to enhance or impede the goals of the tutors?
- What reinforcers were emitted by software? By tutors? With what frequency?

Figure 11.1. The Three-Way Interaction in Tutor Use of Computer Software

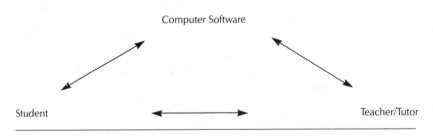

FORMS OF OBSERVATION
USEFUL IN THE COMPUTER ENVIRONMENT

To address the questions, various forms of observation were useful in the computer environment:

1. *Anecdotal Records.* Notes from the teacher/tutors about learning behaviors and interactions with the software were helpful in providing insight into many aspects of the computer situation, such as motivational features of the environment and software characteristics that seemed to enhance or interfere with learning. (One example was, "The printed material is spaced so compactly that it was difficult for David to keep his place.")
2. *Narrative Records.* Recording all aspects of the learning situation from the beginning to the end of the instructional period was useful to understand the context and flow of behavior in the computer environment. As a result, behaviors and events in the computer environment were identified as targets for systematic observational procedures. A major problem noted in the three-way interaction was that when recording one set of events, others were missed.
3. *Rating Scales.* Tutors and students rated the programs along a number of relevant dimensions.
4. *Observation Systems.* Systematic observation procedures were developed to sample and record the frequency of certain behaviors that occurred in the computer-assisted learning environment (see Figure 11.2). Categories of student behavior targeted by the system developed included:

> Attention to and responses directed to the computer screen or keyboard
> Attention to and responses directed to the tutor
> Student or tutor performance of related behavior
> Off-task behaviors

DEVELOPING AN OBSERVATIONAL PROCEDURE
FOR COMPUTER-ASSISTED TUTORING

Steps similar to those outlined in Unit VIII for developing an observational procedure were followed in creating a category system for CATS.

Figure 11.2. Attention Directed to Computer Screen or Keyboard

Eyes on screen	Reading
	Typing input
	Listening to tutor
	Responding to tutor
Eyes on keyboard	Typing input
Eyes off screen	Listening
(attention to tutor)	Commenting
	Responding
	Waiting
Performing related behaviors	
Off task	

In order to develop an appropriate system for observing the three-way interactions, portions of the system developed by Spielvogel and Dunne (1982), "An Observation System for Interaction Analysis of Instructional Computer Software," were reviewed and adapted. This system lists categories of screen presentations, student behaviors, and computer responses. Use of the system helped us attend to and record presentations on the computer and student behaviors. However, since our sample included students with learning difficulties, we were also interested in features of the software and tutor interactions that enhanced or impeded learning. What did tutors do, for example, to make the interaction pedagogically meaningful to the learner?

Attempts at audiotaping proved unsuccessful, due to background noise and the inability of the tape to pick up gestures and modeling behaviors. Videotaping was also not an easy solution, because when the camera was focused on the tutor and screen, some of the learner's behaviors were missed, and vice versa. Furthermore, the screen was frequently blocked by the learner's movements.

The first version of the "Computer-Assisted Tutoring Observation Scan" (Boehm & Brobst, 1982) was developed, considering each component of the CATS triad. Categories were specified for (1) software, (2) learner behaviors, and (3) tutor behaviors. Time-sampling procedures were used to record the occurrence or nonoccurrence of specific target behaviors during a present time interval. The frequency with which behaviors or events occurred within the time interval was ignored.

OUTCOMES OF OBSERVING
COMPUTER-ASSISTED TUTORING

The student, tutor, and computer software were observed during 30-second intervals over a five-minute period, at the beginning of the tutoring session and again for five minutes at the end of the period. This procedure resulted in marking the observation sheet 20 times during each tutoring session. At the point when we had developed this approach, observers were familiar to both the students and their tutors and did not appear to be obtrusive. Using this procedure, we observed students over 30 five-minute intervals for a total of 292 observations. The observed software content included, in order of frequency of observed units, presentations of problems (58.9%), instructions (20.9%), feedback (17.5%), and system messages (2.7%).

Observations of student behaviors indicated that students were highly on task; attention to computer (eyes on screen of keyboard) occurred during 90.5 percent of observed intervals, and attention directed to tutor during another 6.8 percent of the intervals. Off-task behavior occurred during only 3.5 percent of the intervals, an important finding given that tutoring took place in a large room with other people present and other computers in operation. Tutor behaviors were varied. Although tutors were watching students during the greatest portion of observed intervals (38.6%), they also spent time explaining subject matter, providing verbal or physical prompts, reinforcing student efforts, and listening to students (each for 6% or more of the intervals). Tutors and off task 8.2 percent of the intervals, looking around the room or doing some other work.

In addition to the findings generated by this observation instrument, conclusions based on observations were useful concerning other important software characteristics:

- With some programs, an overload of graphics appears, the purpose of which is sometimes unclear.
- Many programs have long, complicated instructions requiring several behavior steps that may be difficult for students to follow.
- The pacing of programs may be too quick, with no way to adjust the pace.
- The unnatural left to right, line-by-line presentation of reading material may make it necessary to eliminate a number of programs.
- The timing of feedback was problematic for a number of learn-

ers. Some programs provided feedback after a predetermined time interval, resulting in feedback occurring at the time the student was figuring out the problem.

In summary, a great deal can be learned from observing the interactions that take place among the student, teacher/tutor, and computer software in computer-assisted learning environments. These observations can serve as a basis for generating teaching strategies, integrating software into remedial programs, creating new software, and adapting existing software to the needs of diverse populations. (See Clements, 1985, for more detailed discussions of the effects of computers on children's learning and development.)

Conclusion

In this book we have highlighted the role that systematic observation in natural settings may play in approaching problems and facilitating educational programs in classroom and other learning environments. Yet the astute observer should not accept naturalistic observation methodology exclusively over other methods of inquiry into educational processes. Although feelings and attitudes underlie many behaviors, it is often impossible to understand these dimensions through direct observation. Interviewing and self-report questionnaires may be more effective means of tapping these areas. For example, evaluating a child's self-esteem might be more directly approached through alternative methods of study. Moreover, since certain behaviors rarely occur in naturalistic situations, it may be necessary to create an experimental or testing situation in order to study — or observe — such behaviors as problem-solving strategies, patterns of discovery, learning, and divergent thinking.

As one of a variety of methodological tools, systematic observation can help the practitioner unravel and understand the complex behavioral exchanges among participants in various learning contexts. Developing and using observation techniques and interpreting the results of systematic observing are complex activities, yet with increased experience, the trained observer will be able to generate useful information on the basis of direct observation.

Furthermore, we would like to suggest that there is no one best way in observing. Each of us must define our own area of concern and choose those methods most appropriate to the problem being confronted as well as to our own style of working. It is hoped that this guide has provided the observer with a flexible yet systematic orientation for collecting and using observational data as vital sources of information in educational decision-making.

Perhaps the most active of all classroom observers is the child. It is well known that children learn what to expect from their teachers and parents, and to a large extent this information is gathered through observing what happens from day to day. Furthermore, observation is essential to children's intellectual and social growth, as they assimilate and accommodate to information from their environment. There is no reason why children should not be guided in the use of systematic observation strategies by defining observation problems, observing objectively, and supporting inferences with data. In fact, such an approach is a curricular emphasis of some recent science education programs.

Carrying this point one step further, why not also train secondary school pupils to help us collect some of the observational data required for making appropriate educational decisions? The next generation of well-trained observers sits in the classroom.

Sample Responses
to Tasks

SAMPLE RESPONSES TO TASK 1

Observations of Your Present Setting

(Five-Minute Time Limit)

Setting: A classroom where students and instructor are gathered.

Time of Day: 2:00 P.M. (Class began at 1:45)

Observer: **A**

Observations in Sequence

1. The room is cold.

2. There are more women than men in this room.

3. I can hear adult voices.

4. There are white cabinets in this room.

5. The blackboard looks gray.

6. Quiet room.

7. Desks give room for work.

8. Area in back for those who want to smoke.

9. Large windows, high ceiling—good ventilation.

10. Age of people seems to range from early 20s to middle 30s.

11. This room seems to be connected to another.

12. Most of the people are busy writing.

Observer: **B**

Observations in Sequence

1. Young teacher.

2. Wooden ledge under blackboard.

3. Faces—some tired, some absorbed.

4. It's quiet.

5. Group is sitting in semicircle.

6. Everyone is looking around and writing.

7. Surprised class is so small.

8. Informal and relaxed atmosphere.

Observer: **C**

Observations in Sequence

1. High ceiling in room.

2. Bright-colored and beige walls.

3. The room is approximately square.

4. Several tables and chairs.

5. A group of about 12 people.

6. Most of the people are busy writing.

7. The room adjoins another where some people are talking.

SAMPLE RESPONSES TO TASK 4

Observations of a Girl in a Nursery Class

Observations Made	Inferences Drawn	Observations Supporting Inferences
1. She is sitting alone on a pile of blocks.	A. The child is not interacting with the other children.	A. 1,2
2. Other children in the block area are not focusing their attention on her.	B. The child is fearful of playing along with active young children.	B. 1,3,4
3. At least two of the four are involved (actively?) in play with blocks.	C. The child is resting briefly after having played with the boys in the block area.	C. 1
4. She is looking away from the other children and their activities. (We do not know what she is looking at.)	D. The child is role-playing an "actress" who has received a bouquet of flowers.	D. 1,5
5. She is holding a bouquet of flowers.		

SAMPLE RESPONSES TO TASK 5

Differentiating Clearly Stated from Poorly Stated Questions

Question	Well Stated	Poorly Stated	Reason
1. Are boys more restless than girls during small-group reading-readiness activities?		✓	What is meant by the word "restless"? The question should be restated to direct the observer's attention to specific behaviors*
2. Does the teacher in this classroom encourage questioning behavior?		✓	What behavior is implied by the word "encourage"? The question should be restated so that "encourage" is more clearly defined in terms of specific behaviors.†
3. During a given kindergarten class day, how many individual children choose to look at a book during free play?	✓		The observer could generate a system for counting the number of children looking at books during the time indicated.
4. Why do the girls in the kindergarten class appear to be more motivated to clean up after snack time?		✓	

*—"Do boys leave their chairs during small-group activities or turn away from the reading-readiness group and appear to attend to other activities more frequently than do girls in this setting?" Or,

—"Does the teacher reprimand boys more frequently than girls during small-group activities?"

†—"How often does the teacher nod, smile, give verbal recognition or other social reinforcers to pupils after they have asked questions?"

*—"Do girls self-initiate cleaning of the table, replacing utensils, etc., more often than boys?"

SAMPLE RESPONSES TO TASK 6

Constraints Imposed by the Setting

Category	Characteristics	Unlikely Behaviors	Likely Behaviors
1. People	Two adults:: one appears to be observing; the other appears to be associated with the group (sex difficult to determine) White and black young boys and girls dressed for warm weather	Behavior reflecting children's social interaction with adults who are older than the two present in the play area	Behavior reflecting children's exchanges with black and white, same-sex and opposite-sex peers and accessible adults Observation of ongoing behavior Children's mobility facilitated by lack of bulky clothing
2. Materials	Hard surface on path Grass 1 wagon, 2 tricycles and 1 tricycle-wagon 1 guitar 3 bushes visible	The lack of typical playground equipment eliminates possibility of activities such as climbing, swinging, sliding	Bicycle-riding, wagon-pulling, unrestricted running and jumping Trying out a guitar and singing Possible games such as "hide and seek"
3. Space	Large open area		Many simultaneous activities
4. Other (Indicate)			

SAMPLE RESPONSES TO TASK 9

Categories	Mutually Exclusive	Overlapping
1. running lying prone sitting in place standing in place	✓	
2. laughing crying talking		✓
3. reading looking listening		✓
4. asking a question giving a command stating an opinion	✓	

In Task 9, examples 1 and 4 are clusters of mutually exclusive categories because an observed behavior could never be classified in more than one of the indicated categories. However, examples 2 and 3 have overlapping categories—an individual can cry and talk simultaneously and, other than in the instance of "reading" braille, one cannot read a book without looking at it.

SAMPLE RESPONSES TO TASK 10

There is some ambiguity as to what constitutes large-muscle coordination, so an observer might ask for a clearer definition, i.e., "A child's playground behavior requiring use of feet, arms, head, and/or body." Even without such a precise definition, one could detail categories of behavior in which "gross-motor" skills are demonstrated. Such a list is given below.

Categories of Large-Muscle Coordination Playground Activity

1. Crawling	6. Running
2. Walking	7. Climbing
3. Jumping	8. Throwing a ball
4. Skipping	9. Riding a bicycle
5. Dancing	10. Other*

*To be specified by the observer at each observation session.

In comparing your list of categories with that given above, you might note that another observer employing your list of categories could observe a behavior that could not be categorized on your list. Therefore, an "Other" category, one which would allow the list of categories to be refined at a later observation session, is necessary in the development of this observation schedule. For example, in using the list given above, a child's playing on a teeter-totter would have to be classified as "Other" because no appropriate category is given. If a list begins to have a large number of "Other" tallies, it would be necessary to revise the list to be more comprehensive.

SAMPLE RESPONSES TO TASK 11

Determining Representative Observational Samples

Problem or Question	Behavior Sample	Representative?		Reasons for Your Response
		Yes	No	
Study of first-grade children's "on task" behavior in school.	Observe the behavior of children sitting in a front-row seat of each row in a particular class.		✔	—Not random sampling: front row might include only children with visual or behavioral problems, etc. —Only one class: this class might not be representative of the entire first-grade population of the school because of achievement group, teacher influence, or other factors.
Count of out-of-seat behaviors of an "acting-out" second grader.	Observe the child on five successive days from 10:00 a.m. to 10:15 a.m.		✔	—One might question five successive days, not necessarily spread out over enough time. —Activities during 10:00 to 10:15 might be the same each day, i.e., only group sessions might have been observed. One needs to sample activities at other times of the day.
Study the extent to which eight-year-old children interact in same-sex, opposite-sex, or mixed-sex groupings on the playground.	Randomly choose four boys and four girls. Observe each child's behavior on a systematic rotation basis for five minutes, indicating the amount of time each child interacts in designated categories. Sampling should be done on different days and at different times.	✔		—Random choice of boys and girls. —Observed on different days to avoid problem of unrepresentative sample of days. —If possible, different times to avoid such factors as fatigue or hunger. —Since interest is in playground interaction only, observation in other settings is eliminated.

References

Adis, W. (1977). A photographic analysis of the classroom environment. New York: Metropolitan School Study Council Exchange, Teachers College, Columbia University, 35 (8).

Ainsworth, M. D. S., Blehar, M., Waters, E., & Wall, S. (1978). *Patterns of attachment*. Hillsdale, NJ: Erlbaum.

Alessi, G. J., & Kay, J. H. (1983). *Behavior assessment for school psychologists*. Kent, OH: National Association of School Psychologists.

Almy, M., & Genishi, C. (1981). *Ways of studying children* (rev. ed.). New York: Teachers College Press.

Altman, L. K. (1980). Emotional state of hostages not clear. *New York Times*, Dec. 29.

American Psychological Association. (1981). *Ethical principles in the conduct of research with human participants*. Washington, DC: American Psychological Association.

Baker, E. H., & Tyne, T. F. (1980, Fall). The use of observational procedures in school psychological services. *School Psychology Monograph, 4* (1), 25–44.

Baldwin, A. L. (1968). *Theories of child development*. New York: Wiley.

Bandura, A., & Walters, R. H. (1963). *Social learning and personality development*. New York: Holt, Rinehart & Winston.

Barker, R. G. (1968). *Ecological psychology*. Stanford: Stanford University Press.

Barker, R. G., & Schoggen, P. (1973). *Qualities of community life*. San Francisco: Jossey-Bass.

Barker, R. G., & Wright, H. F. (1951). *One boy's day: A specimen record of behavior*. New York: Harper & Row.

———. (1955). *Midwest and its children: The psychological ecology of an American town*. New York: Harper & Row.

Baumrind, D. (1968). *Naturalistic observation in the study of parent-child interaction*. Paper presented at 76th Annual American Psychological Association Convention, September.

Beecher, R. (1973). *Teacher approval and disapproval of classroom behavior in prekindergarten, kindergarten, and first grade.* Unpublished doctoral dissertation, Teachers College, Columbia University, New York.

Bersoff, D. N. (1973). Silk purses into sow's ears: The decline of psychological testing and a suggestion for its redemption. *American Psychologist, 28,* 892–899.

Bissell, J. (1973). Planned variation in Head Start and Follow Through. In J. Stanley (Ed.), *Compensatory education for children, ages 2 to 8.* Baltimore: Johns Hopkins University Press.

Bloom, B. S., Hastings, J. T., & Madaus, G. F. (1971). *Handbook on formative and summative evaluation of student learning.* New York: McGraw-Hill.

Boehm, A. (1973). Criterion referenced assessment for the teacher. *Teachers College Record, 75,* 117–126.

Boehm, A. E., & Brobst, K. (1982). *Computer-assisted tutoring observation scan.* Unpublished instrument. New York: Teachers College, Columbia University.

Boehm, A. E., & Slater, B. R. (1981). *Cognitive skills assessment battery* (2nd ed.). New York: Teachers College, Columbia University.

Boice, R. (1983). Observational skills. *Psychological Bulletin, 93* (1), 3–29.

Boyer, E. G., Simon, A., & Karafin, G. R. (Eds.). (1973). Measures of maturation: An anthology of early childhood observation instruments. Philadelphia: Research for Better Schools.

Bracken, B. A. (1982). Observing assessment behavior of preschool children. In K. D. Paget, & B. A. Bracken (Eds.), *The psychoeducational assessment of preschool children.* New York: Grune & Stratton.

Bradley, R. H. (1982). The Home Inventory: A review of the first fifteen years. In N. Anastasiow, W. Frankenburg, & A. Fandal (Eds.), *Identifying the developmentally delayed child.* Baltimore: University Park Press.

Brandt, R. (1972). *Studying behavior in natural settings.* New York: Holt, Rinehart & Winston.

Brison, D. W. (1967). The school psychologist's use of direct observation. *Journal of School Psychology, 5,* 109–115.

Bronfenbrenner, U. (1976, October). The experimental ecology of education. *Educational Researcher,* 5–15.

_____. (1977). Toward an experimental ecology of human development. *American Psychologist, 32,* 513–531.

Brown, R. A. (1973). *First language: The early stages.* Cambridge, MA: Harvard University Press.

Bruner, J., Goodnow, J., & Austin, G. (1956). *A study of thinking.* New York: Wiley.

Caldwell, B. M. (1969). A new "approach" to behavioral ecology. In J. P. Hill (Ed.), *Minnesota symposium on child psychology* (vol. 2). Minneapolis: University of Minnesota Press, 74–109.

Caldwell, B. M., & Bradley, R. H. (1979). *Home observation for measurement of the environment.* Little Rock: Center for Child Development and Education, University of Arkansas at Little Rock.

Cartwright, G. A., & Cartwright, G. P. (1984). *Developing observational skills* (2nd ed.). New York: McGraw-Hill.

Charlesworth, W. (1978). Ethology: Understanding the other half of intelligence. *Social Science Information* (Sage Publications), *17* (2), 231–277.

Clements, D. H. (1985). *Computers in early and primary education.* Englewood Cliffs, NJ: Prentice-Hall.

Cohen, D. H., Stern, V., & Balaban, N. (1983). *Observing and recording the behavior of young children* (3rd ed.). New York: Teachers College Press.

Cone, J. D. (1982). Validity of direct observation assessment procedures. In D. P. Hartmann (Ed.), *Using observers to study behavior.* San Francisco: Jossey-Bass.

Evertson, C. M., & Green, J. L. (1986). Observation as inquiry and method. In M. C. Wittrock (Ed.), *Handbook of research on teaching* (3rd ed.). New York: Macmillan.

Fassnacht, G. (1982). *Theory and practice of observing behaviour.* New York: Academic Press.

Fewell, R. R. (1984). Assessment of preschool handicapped children. *Educational Psychologist, 19* (3), 172–179.

Flanders, N. A. (1965). *Teacher influence, pupil attitudes, and achievement.* U.S. Office of Education, monograph no. 12.

———. (1970). *Analyzing teacher behavior.* Reading, MA: Addison-Wesley.

———. (1975). The use of interaction analyses to study pupil attitudes toward learning. In R. Weinberg, & F. Wood (Eds.), *Observation of pupils and teachers in mainstream and special education settings: Alternative strategies.* Minneapolis U.S.O.E. Leadership Training Institute/Special Education.

Foster, S. I., & Cone, J. D. (1986). Design and use of direct observation procedures. In A. R. Ciminero, K. S. Calhoun, & E. E. Adams

(Eds.), *Handbook of behavioral assessment* (2nd ed.). New York: Wiley.

Gagné, R. M. (1985). *The conditions of learning*. New York: Holt, Rinehart & Winston.

Genishi, C. (1982). Observational research methods for early childhood education. In B. Spodek (Ed.), *Handbook of research in early childhood education*. New York: Free Press, 564–591.

Ginsburg, H. P. (1987). *Assessing the arithmetic abilities and instructional needs of students*. Austin, TX: Pro-Ed.

Gitler, D., & Gordon, R. (1979). Observing and recording young handicapped children's behavior: A comparison among observational methodologies. *Exceptional Children, 2*, 134–135.

Glaser, R., & Nitko, A. J. (1971). Measurement in learning and instruction. In R. L. Thorndike (Ed.), *Educational measurement*. Washington, DC: American Council on Education, 625–670.

Good, T. L., & Brophy, J. E. (1984). *Looking in classrooms* (3rd ed.). New York: Harper & Row.

Gordon, I. J., & Jester, R. E. (1973). Techniques of observing teaching in early childhood and outcomes of particular procedures. In R. M. W. Travers (Ed.), *Second handbook of research on teaching*. Chicago: Rand McNally, 184–217.

Gronlund, N. E. (1985). *Measurement and evaluation in teaching* (5th ed.). New York: Macmillan.

Hartmann, D. P. (1982). Assessing the dependability of observational data. In D. P. Hartmann (Ed.), *Using observers to study behavior*. San Francisco: Jossey-Bass.

Heller, K., Holtzman, W., & Messick, S. (1982). *Placing children in special education: A strategy for equity*. Washington, DC: National Academy Press.

Heller, M. S., & White, M. A. (1975). Rates of teacher approval and disapproval to higher and lower ability classes. *Journal of Educational Psychology, 67*, (6), 796–800.

Hoge, R. D. (1985). The validity of direct observation measures of pupil classroom behavior. *Review of Educational Research, 55* (4), 469–483.

Hollenbeck, A. R. (1978). Problems of reliability in observational research. In G. D. Sackett (Ed.), *Observing behavior, vol. II: Data collection and analyses methods*. Baltimore: University Park Press.

Hunter, C. P. (1977). Classroom observation instruments and teacher inservice training by school psychologists. *School Psychology Monograph, 3* (2), 45–88.

Irwin, D. M., & Bushnell, M. M. (1980). *Observational strategies for child study*. New York: Holt, Rinehart & Winston.

Joyce, B., & Weil, M. (1972). *Models of teaching*. Englewood Cliffs, NJ: Prentice-Hall.

Kagan, J., & Kogan, N. (1970). Individual variation in cognitive processes. In P. H. Mussen (Ed.), *Carmichael's handbook of child psychology*. New York: Wiley.

Kaufman, M., Agard, J. A., & Semmel, M. I. (1985). *Mainstreaming: Learners and their environment*. Cambridge, MA: Brookline Books.

Kazdin, A. E. (1982). Observer effects: Reactivity of direct observation. In D. P. Hartmann (Ed.), *Using observers to study behavior*. San Francisco: Jossey-Bass.

Keller, H. (1986). Behavioral observation approaches to personality assessment. In H. M. Knoff, *The assessment of child and adolescent personality*. New York: Guilford Press, 353–397.

Kent, R. N., & Foster, S. L. (1977). Direct observational procedures: Methodological issues in naturalistic settings. In A. R. Ciminero, K. S. Calhoun, & H. E. Adams (Eds.), *Handbook of behavioral assessment*. New York: Wiley.

Keogh, B. K. (1972). Psychological evaluation of exceptional children: Old hang-ups and new directions. *Journal of School Psychology, 10*, 141–145.

Kerlinger, F. N. (1964 & 1973). *Foundations of behavioral research*. New York: Holt, Rinehart & Winston.

Kleinmuntz, B. (1967). *Personality measurement*. Homewood, IL: Dorsey Press.

Kogan, N. (1983). Stylistic variation in childhood and adolescence: Creativity, metaphor, and cognitive style. In P. H. Mussen (Ed.), *Handbook of child psychology* (4th ed.), (vol. 3, pp. 630–706). New York: Wiley.

Kounin, J. S. (1975). An ecological approach to classroom activity settings: Some methods and findings. In R. A. Weinberg, & F. H. Wood (Eds.), *Observation of pupil and teachers in mainstream and special education settings*. Minneapolis: U.S.O.E. Leadership Training Institute/Special Education.

Kowatrakul, S. (1959). Some behaviors of elementary school children related to classroom activities and subject areas. *Journal of Educational Psychology, 50*, 121–128.

Lambert, N. M., Windmiller, M., Cole, L. S., & Tharinger, D. (1981). *AAMD Adaptive Behavior Scale – school edition*. Monterey, CA: Publishers Test Service, CTB/McGraw-Hill.

Landesman-Dwyer, S., Stein, J. G., & Sackett, G. P. (1978). A behavioral and etiological study of group homes. In G. P. Sackett (Ed.), *Observing behaviors* (Vol. 1: Theory and applications in mental retardation). Baltimore: University Park Press, 349–378.

Lynch, W. W. (1977, Spring). Guidelines to the use of classroom observation instruments by school psychologists. *School Psychology Monograph, 3* (1), 1–22.

Lytton, H. (1971). Observation studies of parent–child interaction: A methodological review. *Child Development, 42,* 651–684.

Martin, J. (1976). Developing category observation instruments for the analysis of classroom behavior. *Classroom Interaction Newsletter, 12* (1), 5–16.

Martuza, V. R. (1977). *Applying norm-referenced and criterion-referenced measurement in education.* Boston: Allyn and Bacon.

Mash, E. J., & McElwee, J. D. (1974). Situational effects on observer accuracy: Behavior predictability, prior experience, and complexity of coding categories. *Child Development, 45,* 367–377.

Masling, J., & Stern, G. (1969). The effect of the observer in the classroom. *Journal of Educational Psychology, 60,* 351–354.

McCutcheon, G. (1981). On the interpretation of classroom observations. *Educational Researcher, 10* (5), 5–10.

McGrew, W. C. (1972). *An ethological study of children's behavior.* New York: Academic Press.

Mead, M. (1932). *Coming of age in Samoa.* New York: Morrow.

Medinnus, R. (1976). *Child study and observation guide.* New York: Wiley.

Medley, D. M., & Mitzel, H. E. (1963). Measuring classroom behavior by systematic observation. In N. L. Gage (Ed.), *Handbook of research in teaching.* Chicago: Rand McNally, 247–328.

Miller, D. (1979). Role of naturalistic observation in comparative psychology. *American Psychologist, 32,* 211–219.

Minnesota Department of Education, Special Education Section (1980). A consideration of the assessment process for handicapped children under five: Observing the behavior of young children and assessing the environments in which they learn. St. Paul: Minnesota Department of Education.

Morine, G. (1975). Interaction analysis in the classroom: Alternative applications. In R. Weinberg, & F. Wood (Eds.), *Observation of pupils and teachers in mainstream and special education settings: Alternative strategies.* Minneapolis: U.S.O.E. Leadership Training Institute/Special Education.

Myklebust, H. R. (1971). *The pupil rating scale.* New York: Grune & Stratton.

O'Leary, K. D., & O'Leary, S. (1972). *Classroom management: The successful use of behavior modification.* New York: Pergamon Press.

Parsons, T., & Bales, R. (1955). *Family socialization and interaction process.* Glencoe, IL: Free Press.

Piaget, J. (1960). *The child's conception of the world.* Patterson, NJ: Littlefield, Adams, & Co.

Popham, W. J. (Ed.). (1971). *Criterion-referenced measurement.* Englewood Cliffs, NJ: Educational Technology Publications.

Resnick, L. B. (1976). Task analysis in instructional design: Some cases from mathematics. In D. Klahr (Ed.), *Cognition and instruction.* Hillsdale, NJ: Erlbaum.

Rheingold, H. L. (1982). Ethics as an integral part of research in child development. In R. Vasta (Ed.), *Strategies and techniques of child study.* New York: Academic Press.

Rosenshine, B., & Furst, N. (1973). The use of direct observation to study learning. In R. M. W. Travers (Ed.), *Second handbook of research on teaching.* Chicago: Rand McNally, 122–183.

Rosenthal, R. (1978). How often are our numbers wrong? *American Psychologist, 33,* 1005–1007.

Rowley, G. L. (1976). The reliability of observational measures. *American Education Research Journal, 13* (1), 51–59.

Rowley, G. L. (1978). The relationship of reliability in classroom research to the amount of observation: An extension of the Spearman-Brown formula. *Journal of Educational Measurement, 15* (3), 165–180.

Russell Sage Foundation. (1969). *Guidelines for the collection, maintenance, and dissemination of pupil records.* New York: Russell Sage Foundation.

Sattler, J. M. (1982). *Assessment of children's intelligence and special abilities* (2nd ed.). Boston: Allyn & Bacon.

Scarr, S., Weinberg, R., & Levine, A. (1986). *Understanding development.* San Diego: Harcourt Brace Jovanovich.

Semmel, M. (1975). Application of systematic classroom observation to the study and modification of pupil–teacher interaction in special education. In R. Weinberg, & F. Wood (Eds.), *Observation of pupils and teachers in mainstream and special education settings: Alternative strategies.* Minneapolis U.S.O.E. Leadership Institute/ Special Education.

Simon, A., & Boyer, E. G. (Eds.). (1967, 1970). *Mirrors for behavior: An anthology of classroom observation instruments* (vols. A & B). Philadelphia: Research for Better Schools.

_____. (1969). Technical tools for teaching. In M. Gottsegen, & G. Gottsegen (Eds.), *Professional school psychology*. New York: Grune & Stratton, 1969.

_____. (Eds.). (1974). *Mirrors for behavior III*. Wyncote, PA: Communications Materials Center.

Sitko, M. C., Fink, A. H., & Gillespie, P. H. (1977, Spring). Utilizing systematic observation for decision making in school psychology. *School Psychology Monograph, 3* (1), 23–44.

Society for Research in Child Development (1982, Winter). Ethical standards for research with children. *Newsletter*, 3–5.

Spache, G., & Spache, E. (1973). *Reading in the elementary school*. Boston: Allyn & Bacon.

Sparrow, S. S., Balla, D. A., & Cichetti, D. V. (1984). *Vineland adaptive behavior scales*. Circle Pines, MN: American Guidance Service.

Spielvogel, B., & Dunne, J. (1982). *Observational system for interaction analysis of computer software*. Unpublished system. New York: Teachers College, Columbia University.

Spindler, G. (1982). *Doing the ethnography of schooling: Educational anthropology in action*. New York: Holt, Rinehart & Winston.

Stallings, J. A. (1977). *Learning to look*. Belmont, CA: Wadsworth.

Strain, P. S., Lambert, D. L., Kerr, M. M., Stagg, V., & Lenkener, D. A. (1983). Naturalistic assessment of children's compliance to teachers' requests and consequences for compliance. *Journal of Applied Behavior Analysis, 16*, 243–249.

Taplin, P. S., & Reid, J. B. (1973). Effects of instructional set and experimenter influence on observer reliability. *Child Development, 44*, 547–554.

Thorndike, R. L., & Hagen, E. P. (1977). *Measurement and evaluation in psychology and education* (4th ed.). New York: Wiley.

Valett, R. E. (1969). *Developmental task analysis*. Belmont, CA: Fearon Publishers.

Vasta, R. (1979). *Studying children*. San Francisco: W. H. Freeman & Co.

Waters, V. (1973). *Teacher differentiated approval and disapproval of boys and girls in the classroom*. Unpublished doctoral dissertation. Teachers College, Columbia University, New York.

Weinberg, R., & Wood, F. (Eds.). (1975). *Observation of pupils and teachers in mainstream and special education settings: Alternative strategies*. Minneapolis: U.S.O.E. Leadership Training Institute/ Special Education.

White, B., Watts, J., Barnett, I., Kaban, B., Marmor, J., & Shapiro, B. (1973b). *Environment and experience: Major influences on the development of the young child*. Englewood Cliffs, NJ: Prentice-Hall.

White, M. A. (1975). Natural rates of teacher approval and disapproval in the classroom. *Journal of Applied Behavior Analysis, 8,* 367–372.

White, M. A., Beecher, R., Heller, M., & Waters, V. (1973a). *Teacher approval/disapproval record*. New York: Teachers College, Columbia University.

Wright, H. F. (1960). Observational child study. In P. H. Mussen (Ed.), *Handbook of research methods in child development*. New York: Wiley.

_____. (1967). *Recording and analyzing child behavior*. New York: Harper & Row.

Bibliography

This bibliography includes general references on the development of observation skills as well as a selected list of observation schedules and systems for observation and recording. The volumes edited by Simon and Boyer (1967, 1970, 1974) and Boyer, Simon, and Karafin (1973) provide a comprehensive survey and classification of numerous observation instruments. These, and other citations from the References, are not included in the Bibliography.

Alberts, P. A., & Troutman, A. C. *Applied behavior analysis for teachers: Influencing student performance.* Columbus, OH: Charles E. Merrill, 1982.

Alvord, J. R. *Home token economy: An incentive program for children and their parents.* Champaign, IL: Research Press, 1973.

Amidon, E., & Hunter, E. (Verbal interaction category system [VICS]). *Improving teaching: The analysis of classroom verbal interaction.* New York: Holt, Rinehart & Winston, 1967.

Arrington, R. E. Time-sampling in studies of social behavior: A critical review of techniques and results with research suggestion. *Psychological Bulletin*, 1943, *40*, 81–124.

Aschner, M. J., & Gallagher, J. (Aschner-Gallagher system). In A. Bellack (Ed.), *Research in Training.* New York: Teachers College Press, 1963; or J. Gallagher, G. Nuthall, & B. Rosensine, *Classroom observation* (AERA Monograph Series on Curriculum Evaluation). Chicago: Rand McNally, 1970, 35–39.

Axline, V. Observing children at play. *Teachers College Record*, 1950–51, *52*, 353–368.

Baldwin, C. P. Naturalistic studies of classroom learning. *Review of Educational Research*, 1965, *35*, 107–113.

Bales, R. F. *Interaction process analysis.* Reading, MA: Addison-Wesley, 1951.

Bales, R. F., & Gerbrands, H. The interaction recorder: An apparatus and checklist for sequential content analysis of social interactions. *Human Relations*, 1948, *1*, 456–463.

Barker, R. G. (Ed.). *The stream of behavior*. New York: Appleton-Century-Crofts, 1963.

Baumrind, A. Approaches to use of observational methods of a study of parent–child interaction. Paper presented at Society for Research in Child Development, Philadelphia: April 1973.

Becker, W. C., Engelmann, S., & Thomas, D. R. *Teaching 1: Classroom management*. Chicago: Science Research Associates, 1975.

Bell, R. Structuring parent–child interaction situations for direct observation. *Child Development*, 1964, *35*, 1009–1020.

Bellack, A. (Ed.). *Theory and research in teaching*. New York: Teachers College Press, 1963.

Biber, B., Murphy, L., Woodcock, L., & Black, I. *Child life in school: A study of a seven year old group*. New York: Dutton, 1942.

Biddle, B. J. Methods and concepts in classoom research. *Review of Educational Research*, 1967, *37*, 337–357.

Blurton-Jones, N. A. (Ed.). *Ethological studies of child behavior*. London: Cambridge University Press, 1972.

_____. Non-verbal communication in children. In R. A. Hinde (Ed.). *Non-verbal communication*. London: Cambridge University Press, 1972, 271–296.

Bower, E. M. *Technical report: A process for in-school screening of children with emotional handicaps*. Princeton, NJ: Educational Testing Service, 1966.

Coller, A. R. *Systems for the observation of classroom behavior in early childhood education*. Urbana, IL: ERIC Clearinghouse on Early Childhood Education, 1972.

Combs, A. W. *The professional education of teachers*. Boston: Allyn & Bacon, 1965.

Emmerich, W. Some theoretical advantages of behavioral observations: Illustrations from a longitudinal study. Paper presented at Society for Research in Child Development, Philadelphia, April 1973.

Evans, E. D. Measurement practices in early childhood education. In R. Colvin & E. Zaffiro (Eds.), *Preschool education: A handbook for the training of early childhood educators*. New York: Springer, 1974.

Feagans, L. Ecological theory as a model for constructing a theory of emotional disturbance. In W. C. Rhodes & M. L. Tracy (Eds.), *A study of child variance, Vol. 1: Conceptual models*. Ann Arbor, MI: Institute for the Study of Mental Retardation and Related Disabilities, 1972, 323–389.

Gagné, R. M. Observations of school learning. *Educational Psychologist*, 1973, *10*, 112–116.

Gallagher, J. A topic classification system in analysis of BSCS concept presentation. *Classroom Interaction Newsletter* (Philadelphia, Research for Better Schools), May 1967, *2*, 12–16.

_____., Nuthall, G., & Rosenshine, B. *Class observation* (AERA Monograph Series on Curriculum Evaluation). Chicago: Rand McNally, 1970.

Gellert, E. Systematic observation: A method of child study. *Harvard Educational Review*, 1955, *25*, 179–195.

Good, T. L., & Brophy, J. E. Teacher-child dyadic interactions: A new method of classroom observation. *Journal of School Psychology*, 1970, *8*, 131–138.

Goodenough, F. The observation of children's behavior as a method in social psychology. *Social Forces*, 1937, *15*, 476–479.

Gordon, I. *Studying the child in school*. New York: Wiley, 1966.

Gump, P. V. *The classroom behavior setting, its nature and relation to student behavior*. Final Report to U.S. Office of Education, Project no. 5-0334, 1967.

Haggerty, M. E., Olson, W. C., & Wickman, E. K. *Haggerty-Olson-Wickman behavior rating schedules*. Yonkers, NY: World Book, 1930.

Hall, R. V., and Hall, M. *How to use time out*. Lawrence, KS: H & H Enterprises, 1980.

Hammill, D. D., & Bartel, N. R. *Teaching children with learning and behavior problems*. Boston: Allyn & Bacon, 1982.

Herbert, J. Observation as a research technique. *Psychology in the Schools*, *1*, 124–135, 1970.

Herbert, J. O., & Attridge, C. A guide for developers and users of observation systems and manuals. *American Educational Research Journal*, 1975, *12*, 1–20.

Hersen, M., & Bellack, A. S. *Behavioral assessment: A practical handbook* (2nd ed.). New York: Pergamon, 1981.

Heyns, R. W., & Lippitt, R. Systematic observation techniques. In G. Lindzey (Ed.), *Handbook of social psychology, Vol. 1: Theory and method*. Cambridge, MA: Addison-Wesley, 1954, 370–404.

Hough, J. B. (Hough System). Interaction analysis in a general methods course. *Classroom Interaction Newsletter*, May 1966. Philadelphia: Research for Better Schools, *1*, 7–10.

Hughes, M. (Hughes System). *Development of the means for the assessment of the quality of teaching in the elementary schools* (U.S. Office of Education, Cooperative Research Project no. 353). Washington, DC: U.S. Office of Education, 1960.

Hutt, S. J., & Hutt, C. *Direct observation and measurement of behavior*. Springfield, IL: Thomas, 1970.

Jersild, A. T., & Meigs, M. F. Direct observation as a research method. *Review of Education Research*, 1939, 9, 472–482.

Jones, R. R., Reid, J. B., & Patterson, G. R. Naturalistic observation in clinical assessment. In P. McReynolds (Ed.), *Advances in psychological assessment* (vol. 3). San Francisco: Jossey-Bass, 1975, 42–95.

Kazdin, A. E. *Behavior modification in applied settings* (rev. ed.). Homewood, IL: Dorsey Press, 1980.

Lambert, N. M., Cox, H. W., & Hartsough, C. S. The observability of intellectual functioning of first graders. *Psychology in the Schools*, 1970, 7, 74–85.

Lewin, K. Psychological ecology. In D. Cartwright (Ed.), *Field theory in social science: Selected theoretical papers by Kurt Lewin*. New York: Harper & Row, 1951, 170–187.

Martin, G., & Pear, J. *Behavior modification: What it is and how to do it* (2nd ed.). Englewood Cliffs, NJ: Prentice-Hall, 1983.

Mattick, I., & Perkin, F. J. *Guidelines for observation and assessment: An approach to evaluating a learning environment of a daycare center*. Washington, DC: Daycare and Child Development Council of America, 1973.

Mehrabian, A. Some referents and measures of non-verbal behavior. *Behavior Research Methods and Instrumentation*, 1969, 1, 203–207.

Melbin, M. Field methods and techniques: An interaction recording device for participant observers. *Human Organization*, 1954, 13, 29–33.

Moos, R. H. Conceptualizations of human environments. *American Psychologist*, 1973, 28, 652–665.

Morris, R. J. *Behavior modification with exceptional children*. Glenview, IL: Scott, Foresman, 1985.

Openshaw, M. K., & Cyphert, F. (Taxonomy of Teacher Behavior). *Development of a taxonomy for the classification of teacher classroom behavior*. Columbus: Ohio State University Research Foundation, 1966.

Patterson, G. R. *Living with children: New methods for parents and teachers*. Champaign, IL: Research Press, 1976.

Perkins, H. A procedure for assessing the classroom behavior of students and teachers. *American Educational Research Journal*, 1964, 1, 249–260.

Randhawa, B. S., & Fu, L. W. Assessment and effect of some classroom environment variables. *Review of Educational Research*, 1973, 43, 303–322.

Riskin, J. Family interaction scales: A preliminary report. *Archives of General Psychiatry*, 1964, *11*, 484–494.

Rowen, B. J. *The children we see: An observational approach to child study*. New York: Holt, Rinehart & Winston, 1973.

Rutter, M. A. A children's behavior questionnaire for completion by teachers: Preliminary findings. *Journal of Child Psychology and Psychiatry*, 1967, *8*, 1–11.

Ryans, D. *Characteristics of teachers*. Washington, DC: American Council on Education, 1960.

Sackett, G. P. (Ed.). *Observing behavior* (2 vols.). Baltimore: University Park Press, 1978.

Schalock, H. D., & Hale, J. (Eds.). *A competency based, field-centered systems approach to elementary teacher education, Vol. 1: Overview and specifications*. Portland, OR: Northwest Regional Educational Research Laboratory, 1968.

Semmel, M., & Thiagarajan, S. Observation systems and the special education teacher. *Focus on Exceptional Children*, 1973, *5*, 1–12.

Shure, M. B. Psychological ecology of a nursery school. *Child Development*, 1963, *34*, 979–992.

Simon, A., & Agazarian, Y. *Sequel analysis of verbal interaction (SAVI)*. Philadelphia: Research for Better Schools, 1967.

Soar, R. S., Soar, R. M., & Ragosta, M. *The Florida climate and control system (FLACCS)*. Gainesville, FL: Institute for Development of Human Resources, College of Education, University of Florida, 1971.

Spaulding, R. (Coping Analysis Schedule for Educational Settings [CASES]). *An introduction to the use of the coping analysis schedule for educational settings and S-T-A-R-S*. Durham, NC: Education Improvement Program, Duke University, 1967.

——————. (Spaulding Teacher Activity Rating Schedule [STARS]). *An introduction to the use of C-A-S-E-S and STARS*. Durham, NC: Education Improvement Program, Duke University, 1967.

Weick, K. Systematic observational methods. In G. Lindzey & E. Aronson (Eds.), *Handbook of social psychology, Vol. 2, Research methods*. Reading, MA: Addison-Wesley, 1968, 357–451.

Westbury, I., & Bellack, A. (Eds.). *Research into classroom processes*. New York: Teachers College Press, 1971.

White, O. R., & Haring, N. G. *Exceptional teaching*. Columbus, OH: Charles E. Merrill, 1980.

Willems, P., & Raush, H. L. (Eds.). *Naturalistic viewpoints in psychological research*. New York: Holt, Rinehart & Winston, 1968.

Withall, J. Observing and recording behavior. *Review of Educational Research*, 1960, *30*, 496–512.

_____. Evaluation of classroom climate. *Childhood Education*, 1969, *45*, 403–408.

Wrightstone, J. W. Observational techniques. In C. W. Harris & M. R. Liba (Eds.), *Encyclopedia of educational research* (3rd ed.) New York: Macmillan, 1960, 927–933.

Index

AAMD (American Association on Mental Deficiency), 13
Adaptive Behavior Scale — Public School Version (AAMD), 13
Adis, W., 110
Affective observational system, 52, 53
Agard, J. A., 13
Agreement, observer, 63–65, 64 (fig.)
Ainsworth, M. D. S., 9
Alessi, G., 12, 78
Almy, M., 10
American Association on Mental Deficiency (AAMD), 13
American Psychological Association, 91
Anecdotal records, 16–17, 78
in computer environment, 117
Anthropologists, 7
Approval records, *see* TAD
Attachment patterns in infancy, study of, 9
Audio recordings, *see* Tape recording equipment
Austin, G., 13

Baby biographies, 8
Baker, E. H., 12, 64, 67, 68, 69
Balaban, N., xiv, 10
Baldwin, A. L., 10
Bales, R., 7
Bandura, A., 10
Barker, R. G., 7, 8, 18, 41
Baumrind, D., 9
Beecher, R., 9, 10, 76

Behavior
context of, 46, 48 (fig.), 50
defining, 51, 52–53
knowing and defining, 52–53
labeling, 51–53
making categories exhaustive, 54–56
mutually exclusive categories, 53–54, 55
recording, 79–86
sampling, 71–79
setting limits in categorizing, 54
specifying categories, 56–57
Behavioral information testing, observation and, 12–13
Behavior management, observation in, 10–11
Bersoff, D. N., 10
Bias
observee, 68–69
observer, 67–68
Biographies, 8
Black and white media in observation, 113
Blehar, M., 9
Bloom, B. S., 14
Boehm, A. E., 14, 21, 22, 118
Boice, R., 68
Boyer, E. G., 52–53, 81, 81 n, 82, 91
Bradley, R. H., 9
Brainstorming categories, 60
Brandt, R., 91
Brobst, K., 118
Bronfenbrenner, U., 7
Brophy, J. E., xiv, 15, 67

Brown, R. A., 8
Bruner, J., 13

Caldwell, B. M., 9
Cartwright, G. A., 17
Categories of behavior
  broadly defined, 57
  in classroom observation, 102–103
  developing, 60–61
  exhaustive, making, 54–56
  mutually exclusive, 53–54, 55
  narrowly defined, 57
  number used in sampling, 78
  setting limits, 54
  specifying, 56–57
Category systems, 58, 59 (fig.), 60
  and Sample Worksheet A, 83
Category System Sample Worksheet,
  58, 59 (fig.)
Central tendency, error of, 23
Charlesworth, W., 9
Checklists, 20
Child development, techniques of
  observation in studying, 8–10
Children's developmental differences,
  97–100
Child's privacy, 91
Classroom climate, running records
  of, 2–3, 18
Classroom interaction analysis, 15
Classroom observations, steps to
  making, 100–106
Classroom paraprofessionals, 93–94
Classroom problems, solving through
  observational techniques, 95–97,
  96 (fig.), 98 (fig.)
Cognitive development of children,
  observation in, 8
Cognitive observational system, 52,
  53
Cognitive Skills Assessment Battery,
  21
Cohen, D. H., xiv, 10
Color media in observation, 113

Computer analysis of observational
  data, 9
Computer-assisted learning environ-
  ment, observation methods for,
  115–120
Computer-assisted tutoring, 116
  observational procedure for,
  117–118
  outcomes of, 119
Computer-Assisted Tutoring Scan,
  118
Computer-Assisted Tutoring Service
  (CATS), 116, 117–118
Computers in recording behavior, 113
Concurrent validity, 88
Cone, J. D., 63 n, 65, 78, 88 n, 114
Consensual drift, 68
Construct validity, 89
Content validity, 89
Controlled experiments, 6–7
Coping strategies, study of, 11, 13
Counting devices, 113
Criterion-referenced assessment,
  observation and, 14–15
Cultural norms, observation and, 4
Curriculum effectiveness
  determining, 95–97, 96 (fig.), 98
    (fig.)
  observing, 15

Descriptive phrases in rating scales,
  21
Developmental differences in
  children, 97–100
Developmental influences, observa-
  tion and, 4
Developmental Task Analysis, 21
Diary description, 8, 16
Direct viewing, advantages and
  disadvantages of, 109–110
Disapproval records, see TAD
Dunne, J., 119
Duration recording, 77–78

Early childhood arena, observing in, 2–3
Ecological approach to studying phenomena, 7–8, 9
Educational environment, observation within, 10–15
Educational program effectiveness, determining, 95–97, 96 (fig.), 98 (fig.)
Education for All Handicapped Children Act of 1975 (Public Law 94–142), 14
Electronic learning environment, observation methods for, 115–120
Equipment intrusiveness, observee reliability and, 69
Error of central tendency, 23
Error of leniency, 23
Error of severity, 23
Ethical Principles in the Conduct of Research with Human Participants (APA), 92
Ethical Standards for Research with Children, 92
Ethics in observation, 69, 91–92
Ethological research, 8–9
Event sampling, 75–76, 75 (fig.)
  in classroom observation, 103–104
  versus time sampling, 76–77, 76 (fig.)
Evertson, C. M., 83, 91, 115
Exceptional children, observation in assessment of, 13
Experiments, controlled, 6–7

Fassnacht, G., 67
Fewell, R. R., 20
Fink, A. H., 12
First-hand observation, advantages and disadvantages of, 109–110
Flanders, N. A., 15, 58, 81, 81 n
Flanders Interaction Analysis Categories, 15, 58, 74, 81–82, 81 (fig.)

Formal observation schedules, 23–24
Forms of observation, 16–24
  anecdotal records, 16–17
  checklists, 20
  diary descriptions, 16
  formal observation schedules, 23–24
  rating scales, 20–23
  specimen records, 17–20
Foster, S. I., 63 n, 65, 78, 88 n, 113, 114

Gagné, R. M., 15, 60
Galileo Galilei, 6
Genishi, C., 10
Gillespie, P. H., 12
Ginsburg, H. P., 13, 112
Gitler, D., 13
Glaser, R., 15
Good, T. L., xiv, 15, 67
Goodnow, J., 13
Gordon, I. J., 91
Gordon, R., 13
Green, J. L., 83, 91, 115
Gronlund, N. E., 15

Hagen, E. P., 17
Halo effect, 23, 67, 94–95
Hartmann, D. P., 63 n, 64, 68
Hastings, J. T., 14
Hearing-impaired children, observation in assessment of, 13
Heller, M., 9, 10, 14, 76
Heller, M. S., 10
Herbert, J., 66
Hollenbeck, A. R., 63n
Holtzman, W., 14
HOME (Home Observation for Measurement of the Environment), 9
Hypotheses
  generation of, 6
  and observer reliability, 67

Individual perceptions, 4
Individuals
  within the setting, describing and
    observing, 45
  visible characteristics of, 45, 47
Inferences
  drawing, 32–36
  and valid observations, 87–88
Informed consent, 92
Institutionalized children, observation
  in assessment of, 13
Interaction analysis, 15
Interpretations, valid observations
  and, 87–88
Interval recording, 77–78
Invasion of privacy, 91
Iranian hostage crisis (1980), 112

Jester, R. E., 91
Joyce, B., 15

Kagan, J., 13
Karafin, G. R., 91
Kaufman, M., 13
Kaye, J. H., 12, 78
Kazdin, A. E., 67
Kent, R. N., 63 n, 65, 67, 113
Keogh, B. K., 10, 13
Kerlinger, F. N., 21, 23, 52, 54
Kleinmuntz, B., 45 n
Kogan, N., 13
Kounin, J. S., 112
Kowatrakul, S., 79

L,O,U coding system, 72–74, 73 (fig.)
Labeling behaviors, dimensions for,
  51–53
Laboratory-based research in
  development, 9
Laboratory-controlled experiments,
  6–7
Landesman-Dwyer, S., 9

Language acquisition by children,
  observation in, 8
Learning ability, diagnostic assess-
  ment of, 99–100
Learning theory, observation and, 10
Length of observation period, 66
Leniency, error of, 23
Levine, A., 8
Lynch, W. W., 9, 12

Madaus, G. F., 14
Mainstreaming, observation in
  assessment of, 13
Martin, J., 61
Martuzza, V. R., 15
Masling, J., 32
McCutcheon, G., 88
McGrew, W. C., 9
Mead, M., 7
Media and observation, 107–114
advantages and disadvantages of,
  109–114
mechanics of, 107–108
Medley, D. M., 58, 78
Mentally retarded children, observa-
  tion in assessment of, 13
Messick, S., 14
Mirrors for Behavior (Simon &
  Boyer), 53, 91
Mitzel, H. E., 58, 78
Motion pictures in observation, 108,
  111–113
Mutually exclusive categories, 53–54
  distinguishing, 54, 55
Mutual relationship between people
  and environment, 41
Myklebust, H. R., 21

Narrative records in computer
  environment, 117
Naturalistic approach in studying
  development, 9
Nitko, A. J., 15

Nonoccuring behavior, 64
time sampling and, 71
Norm-referenced testing, 14–15
Number of observations, 66
Numerical judgments in rating scales,
21

Objectivity in observation, aiming
for, 28–31
Observation
within educational environment,
10–15
as method of inquiry, 6–8
techniques of, in studying child
development, 8–10
Observation schedules
in classroom observation, 104
formal, 23–24
Observation skills
application of, 6–15
overview of, 1–5
Observation systems
appropriateness of, 89, 90 (fig.)
in computer environment, 117
as source of errors, 70
Observee bias, 68–69
Observee reactivity, 69
Observer agreement, 63–65, 64 (fig.)
Observer bias, 67–68
Observer drift, 68, 70 (fig.)
Observer reliability, 62–63, 63 (fig.)
Observer's presence, effect of, 31–32
Observer training, inadequate, and
reliability, 68
*Observing and Recording the
Behavior of Young Children*
(Cohen, Stern & Balaban), 10
Occuring behavior, 64
time sampling and, 71
O'Leary, K. D., 10
O'Leary, S., 10
One Boy's Day (Barker & Wright), 7,
18, 41 n
One-way mirrors, 69

Ontario Institute for Studies in
Education, 66
Overview of observation skills, 1–5

Parent-child interactions, study of, 9
Parsons, T., 7
Peer interaction, study of, 12
Perceptions, individual, 4
Personal bias/expectation, observer
reliability and, 67
Pestalozzi, Johann, 8
Photographs in observation, 108,
110–111
Physically-disabled children, observa-
tion in assessment of, 13
Physical setting, observing and
describing, 42, 44
see also Setting
Piaget, J., 4, 8
Point-time sampling, 79
Popham, W. J., 15
Predictive validity, 89
Prejudice, 67
Preschool Behavior Questionnaire, 13
Previewing categories, 60–61
Privacy, invasion of, 91–92
Problem definition in observation,
38–39
in classroom observation, 100–101
Problem-solving strategies, study of,
11, 13
Psychoeducational assessment,
observation in, 11–14
Public Law 94–142 (Education for
All Handicapped Children Act of
1975), 14
Pupil Rating Scale, The, 21
Pupil sampling, 78–79

Questions, differentiating clearly
stated from poorly stated, 39, 40

Rating scales, 20–23
  in computer environment, 117
  descriptive phrases, 21
  examples of ratings used during
    assessment, 22 (fig.)
  numerical judgments, 21
Reactivity, observee, 69
Reading comprehension tests, 13
Reading-impaired children, observa-
    tion in assessment of, 13
Recording observational data, 79–86
  in classroom observation, 104, 105
    (fig.)
  Flanders system, 81–82, 81 (fig.)
  mechanical systems, 113–114
  Sample Worksheet A, 83–84, 83
    (fig.)
  Sample Worksheet B, 85–86, 85
    (fig.)
Reid, J. B., 67
Reinforcing behavior, study of,
    observation and, 10
Reliability, 53
Reliability, observer, 62–63, 63 (fig.)
Reliable observations
  challenges to, 67–70
  in classroom observation, 104
  obtaining, 62–66
  summary checklist for making, 70
    (fig.)
Rheingold, H. L., 92
Rowley, G. L., 65, 66
Running records of classroom
    climate, 2–3, 18
Russell Sage Foundation, 91

Sackett, G. P., 9
Sampling behavior, 71–79
  in classroom observation, 103–104
  duration recording, 77
  event sampling, 75, 75 (fig.)
  interval recording, 77
  number of behavior categories
    used, 78

point-time sampling, 79
  representativeness of behavior
    sample, 78, 79
  and sampling pupils, 79
  time sampling, 71–74, 73 (fig.)
  time versus event sampling, 76–77,
    76 (fig.)
Sattler, J. M., 13
Scarr, S., 8
Schoggen, P., 7, 8
Scientific observation, 6
Selective nature of observations,
    25–36
  inferences, drawing, 32–36
  objectivity, aiming for, 28–31
  observer's presence, effect of, 31–32
  subjectivity, 25, 27–28
Self-concept, 51
Self-help skills
  defining, 14
  event sampling and, 75, 75 (fig.)
Semmel, M. I., 13
Setting
  characteristics of, in classroom
    observation, 101
  components of, in classroom
    observation, 101–102
  components of, analyzing, 42,
    44–45, 46, 48 (fig.), 49
  constraints of the, 39, 41–42, 43
  individuals within, observing and
    describing, 45
  overall physical, observing and
    describing, 42, 44
  tangible materials, observing and
    describing, 44
Severity, error of, 23
Sex differences in verbal approval and
    disapproval, 11
Sign systems, 58, 59 (fig.), 60
  and Sample Worksheet A, 83
Sign System Sample Worksheet, 58,
    59 (fig.)
Simon, A., 52–53, 81, 81 n, 82, 91
Sitko, M. C., 12

Slater, B. R., 21, 22
Slides in observation, 108, 110–111
Social sciences, scientific method in, 6
Society for Research in Child Development, 92
Sociologists, 7
Spache, E., 13
Spache, G., 13
Special education requirements, observation in assessment of, 13
Specimen records, 17–20
Spielvogel, B., 119
Spindler, G., 15
Stability coefficient, 65
Stability of observations, 65–66
Stein, J. G., 9
Stern, G., 32
Stern, V., xiv, 10
Still photographs in observation, 108, 110–111
Subjectivity in observation, 25, 27–28
Summarizing characteristics, 45, 48
Swayze, J. L., 107 n
Systematic observing, 4–5

TAD (Teacher Approval and Disapproval Observation Record), 10–11, 76, 77, 77 (fig.)
Tangible materials, observing and describing, 44
Tape recording equipment, 111
    ethical use of, 91
    intrusiveness of, 69, 111
Taplin, P. S., 67
Task analysis, 20
Task-analyzing categories, 60–61
Teacher Approval and Disapproval Observation Record (TAD), 10–11, 76, 77, 77 (fig.)
Teacher as observer, 93–95
    diagnostic assessment of learning activity, 99–100
    effectiveness of educational

    programs and curricula, 95–97, 96 (fig.), 98 (fig.)
    problems encountered, 94–95
    solving classroom problems through observation techniques, 95–97, 96 (fig.), 98 (fig.)
    studying developmental differences in children, 97–100
Teaching practices, observing, 15
Team teaching, 93–94
Techniques of observation
    to solve classroom problems, 95–97, 96 (fig.) 98 (fig.)
    in studying child development, 8–10
Thorndike, R. L., 17
Time sampling, 71–74, 73 (fig.)
    in classroom observation, 103–104
    coding system for, 72, 74
    Procedure A, 72–74, 73 (fig.)
    Procedure B, 74, 73 (fig.)
    versus event sampling, 76–77, 76 (fig.)
Time-sampling system, 63
Token reinforcement system, 95
Tyne, T. F., 12, 64, 67, 68, 69

Valid observations, making 86–89
    interpretations, 87–88
    types of validity, 88–89
Vasta, R., 64
Verbal behaviors, Flanders categories of, 58, 81, 82 (fig.)
Video equipment
    advantages and disadvantages of, in observation, 111–113
    ethical use of, 91
    intrusiveness of, 69
Vineland Social Maturity Scale, 13

Wall, S., 9
Walters, R. H., 10

Waters, E., 9
Waters, V., 9, 10, 76
Ways of Studying Children (Almy &
    Genishi), 10
Wechsler Intelligence Scale for
    Children — Revised, 89

Weil, M., 15
Weinberg, R., 8
White, M. A., 9, 10, 76, 77
Wright, H. F., 7, 16, 17, 18, 41 n,
    71-72